# Writing Skills

## Grade 6

Flash Kids

Spark Publishing

Harcourt
Family Learning™

Copyright © 2006 by Spark Publishing
Adapted from *Experiences with Writing Styles Grade 6*
Copyright © 1998 by Steck-Vaughn Company
and *Writing Skills Grade 6*
Copyright © 2003 by Steck-Vaughn Company
Licensed under special arrangement with Harcourt Achieve.

Illustrated by Judy Stead

ISBN-13: 978-1-4114-0483-0
ISBN-10: 1-4114-0483-1

For more information, please visit *www.flashkidsbooks.com*
Please submit changes or report errors to *www.flashkidsbooks.com/errors*

Printed and bound in China

**Spark Publishing**
120 Fifth Avenue
New York, NY 10011

# Dear Parent,

Reading and writing well are essential tools for success in all school subjects. In addition, many states now include writing assessments in their standardized tests. There may be no precise formula for good writing, but through studying samples and practicing different styles, your child will build the skills and versatility to approach any writing assignment with ease and confidence.

Each of the six units in this fun, colorful workbook focuses on a unique type of writing that your sixth-grader may be required to use in school or may wish to pursue in his or her free time. These types include personal narrative, how-to writing, descriptive writing, comparative writing, persuasive writing, and short report. The first half of each unit reinforces writing aspects such as putting ideas in a sequence, using descriptive details, working with a thesaurus, and using proofreading marks, in addition to providing fun, inspirational writing ideas for your child to explore alone or with a friend. The second half of each unit focuses on a practice paper that exemplifies the writing type. After your child reads the practice paper, he or she will analyze it, prepare a writing plan for his or her own paper, write a first draft, revise it, and, lastly, allow you or a friend to score it.

Here are some helpful suggestions for getting the most out of this workbook:

- Provide a quiet place to work.
- Go over the directions together.
- Encourage your child to do his or her best.
- Check each activity when it is complete.
- Review your child's work together, noting good work as well as points for improvement.

As your child completes the units, help him or her maintain a positive attitude about writing. Provide writing opportunities such as a journal, in which your child can write about things that happen each day and can keep a running list of topics or story ideas for future writing projects. Read your child's stories aloud at bedtime, and display his or her writing in your home.

Most importantly, enjoy this time you spend together. Your child's writing skills will improve even more with your dedication and support!

# Proofreading Marks

Use the following symbols to help make proofreading faster.

| MARK | MEANING | EXAMPLE |
|------|---------|---------|
| ⬭ | spell correctly | I ⟨liek⟩ dogs. *like* |
| ⊙ | add period | They are my favorite kind of pet⊙ |
| ? | add question mark | Are you lucky enough to have a dog ? |
| ⹀ | capitalize | My dog's name is <u>s</u>cooter. |
| ꝫ | take out | He is a great companion for me and my m̶y̶ family. |
| ∧ | add | We got Scooter when ∧ was eight weeks old. *he* |
| / | make lowercase | My U̸ncle came over to take a look at him. |
| ∿ | switch | He watched the puppy run ⌿in⟍ ⟨around⟩ circles. |
| ∧, | add comma | "Jack ∧, that dog is a real scooter!" he told me. |
| ᐯ ᐯ | add quotation marks | ᐯScooter! That's the perfect name! ᐯ I said. |
| ¶ | indent paragraph | ¶ Scooter is my best friend in the whole world. He is not only happy and loving but also the smartest dog in the world. Every morning at six o'clock, he jumps on my bed and wakes me with a bark. Then he brings me my toothbrush. |

# Table of Contents

# UNIT 1: Personal Narrative

## HOW MUCH DO YOU KNOW?

**Read the personal narrative below. Then answer the questions that follow.**

My Uncle Mike is my hero. When he was seventeen, a fire broke out in his apartment building. As smoke billowed from the building, firefighters kept the neighbors at a safe distance. Suddenly, Uncle Mike heard the cries of a baby. He said that he didn't think, he just broke through the crowd and rushed into the burning building. Then he crawled up the stairs to try to stay below the smoke. He broke down the door of the apartment. Outside, the family stood in frightened silence. Finally, Mike appeared at the apartment window with the baby in his arms. He climbed out the window. Firefighters put up a ladder and helped Uncle Mike and the baby down. My mother hurried to them. She wept as she hugged both Mike and the baby, because that baby was me, her healthy son!

1. From what point of view is this narrative told?

    This story is told by Uncle Mike's nephew.

2. List the event that happened at the beginning of the narrative.

    A fire broke out in a apartment building.

**Complete the chain diagram below as the writer might have done when planning to write this narrative.**

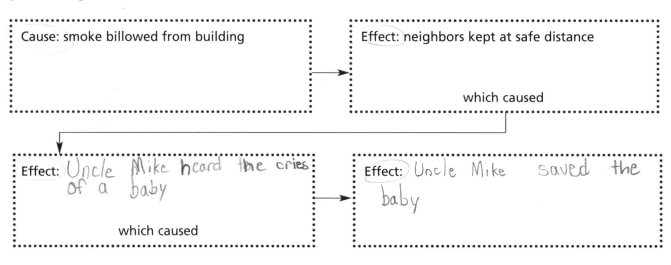

Cause: smoke billowed from building

Effect: neighbors kept at safe distance

which caused

Effect: Uncle Mike heard the cries of a baby

which caused

Effect: Uncle Mike saved the baby

# Analyzing a Personal Narrative

> **A PERSONAL NARRATIVE**
> - is written in the first-person point of view
> - usually reveals the writer's feelings
> - has a beginning, a middle, and an end

**Read the personal narrative below. Then answer the questions that follow.**

The family birthday party began as usual. First, my family gathered with my presents after dinner. I was excited, but I thought I knew what I was getting. My parents had never been able to surprise me.

After I had opened one gift, I heard a faint rustling noise. I paused for a moment, but I heard nothing more. A minute later, I noticed that a large box moved! It was creepy! I jumped to my feet in alarm.

Laughing, my father then picked up the moving present. The box had no bottom at all. A fluffy white kitten was curled up where the present had been. I was finally surprised–with the best birthday present I had ever received.

1. From what point of view is this narrative told? *This story is told by the familys child.*
   What words are clues to this point of view? *family and father*

2. How did the writer feel at the beginning of the narrative?
   *The writer felt that he knew everything that was going to happen.*

3. How did the writer's feelings change by the end of the narrative?
   *His feelings changed because he became suprised after the gift.*

4. List the events of the narrative in the order in which they happened.
   Write a signal word or phrase if one is given for each event.

   a. *The party began*
   b. *I knew what I was going to get*
   c. *I heard a noise*
   d. *A box moved it was creepy.*
   e. *The best present ever*

# Connecting Cause and Effect

TO WRITE A PERSONAL NARRATIVE, GOOD WRITERS
- look for cause-and-effect connections among events
- build stories around cause-and-effect chains

Read the personal narrative below. Look for cause-and-effect relationships around which the writer built the story.

Hot winds from the desert had raised the temperature to 100 degrees. To escape the heat, thousands of people headed for the beach. The road to the beach was soon jammed with cars. The traffic slowed to a crawl. Stop-and-go driving in the heat caused many cars to overheat. Traffic was backed up for miles.

Luce's Juices is located at the side of the road that leads to the beach. People began to pull off the road and come into the juice bar. Hundreds of people decided they would rather wait in an air-conditioned juice bar than in the line of motionless cars. Some people liked the juices so well that they now stop every time they drive by. Because so many people discovered Luce's Juices that day, business has been great ever since.

**Complete the chain diagram below as the writer might have done when planning to write this narrative. One example is done for you.**

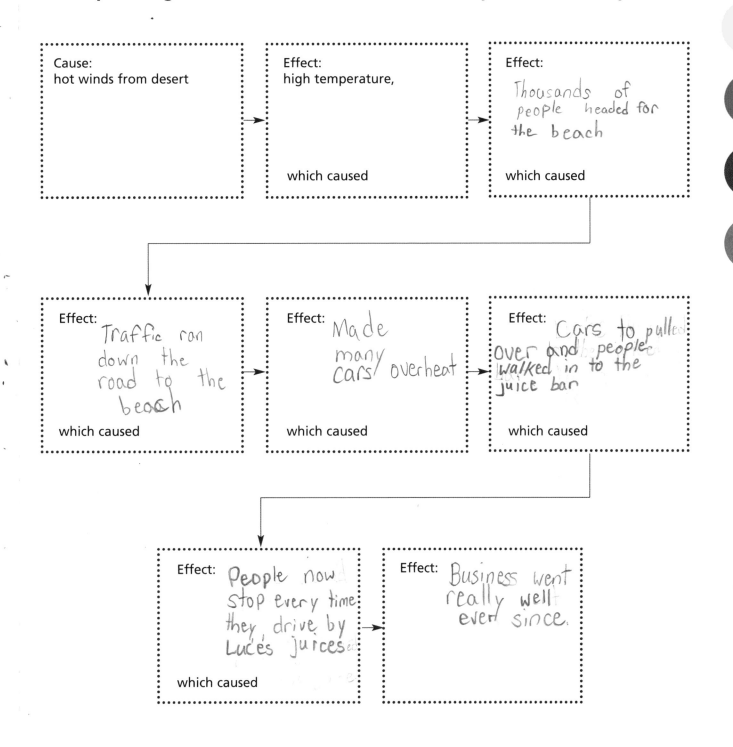

Cause:
hot winds from desert

Effect:
high temperature,

which caused

Effect:
Thousands of people headed for the beach

which caused

Effect:
Traffic ran down the road to the beach

which caused

Effect: Made many cars/ overheat

which caused

Effect: Cars to pulled over and people walked in to the juice bar

which caused

Effect: People now stop every time they drive by Luce's juices

which caused

Effect: Business went really well ever since.

# Using Examples

> Good writers give a reader enough information by using
> - effective examples
> - the right number of examples

Read the following paragraphs. Label each paragraph as having the *right number* of examples, *too many*, or *too few*. If the paragraph has too few examples, write the examples you would add. If the paragraph has too many, write the examples that are not effective.

1.  Wayne was a forgetful person. He was always leaving books on buses and benches. He often forgot to take his homework assignment home. When he did remember, he forgot to bring his completed assignment back to school. On those few occasions when he did bring a completed assignment back to school, Wayne usually forgot to turn it in.

_____

_____

2.  That day everything went wrong for me. My breakfast was burned. My mother refused to buy me a horse. My hair would not go right. I had to iron my shirt. The dog chewed up my homework. I studied the wrong pages for my test. Joan won the spelling bee, and I only came in second. Worst of all, Wayne was assigned as my partner for the oral science report.

_____

_____

3. Working with Wayne, however, turned out better than I thought. He came up with some good ideas for our report.

_____

_____

# Using a Thesaurus

Good writers sometimes use a thesaurus to find
the exact words they need.

**Rewrite each sentence. Use a thesaurus to replace the underlined word.**

1. The Ross family left their <u>home</u> early.

   The Ross family left their living quarters early.

2. The children climbed into the car <u>eagerly</u>.

   The children climbed into the car at once.

3. Bill Ross was the <u>driver</u> for the first thirty minutes.

   Bill Ross was the chauffeur for the first thirty minutes.

4. He had just finished a <u>class</u> in driving at school.

   He had just finished a course in drive at school.

5. Bill and his father <u>changed</u> places before they reached the mountains.

   Bill and his father flipped places before they reached the mountains.

6. The <u>smell</u> of pines was everywhere.

   The fragrance of pines was everywhere.

7. Bill and Susan immediately went for a <u>walk</u>.

   Bill and Susan immediately went for a hike.

# Proofreading a Personal Narrative

> ## PROOFREADING HINT
>
> To be a good proofreader, look for one type of error at a time. For example, proofread once for capitalization errors, once for punctuation errors, and once for spelling errors.

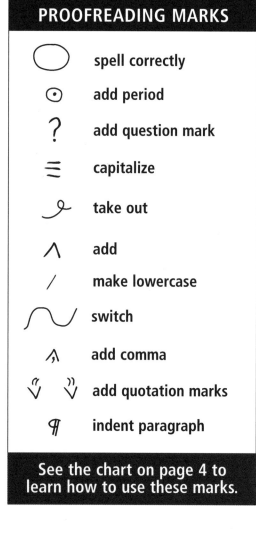

## PROOFREADING MARKS

| | |
|---|---|
| ◯ | spell correctly |
| ⊙ | add period |
| ? | add question mark |
| ≡ | capitalize |
| ℓ | take out |
| ∧ | add |
| / | make lowercase |
| ∿ | switch |
| ⋏ | add comma |
| ⌄ ⌄ | add quotation marks |
| ¶ | indent paragraph |

**See the chart on page 4 to learn how to use these marks.**

Proofread the beginning of the personal narrative, paying special attention to spelling. Use the Proofreading Marks to correct at least eight errors.

What an amazing experience my brothers and I had with the wind last autunm! *autumn* We had driven with our parents to Point Reyes, north of San francisco. Point Reyes is known as one of the windyest *windiest* spots in the cuontry, *country* and on that day the winds were raging up to 50 miles an hour all along the California coast.

I had no way of determining the speed of the wind at Point reyes that afternoon. I can only tell you that when we jumped into the air, we were

blown a full five feet before landing. The wind picked us up and carried us

with the force of (rushhing) water. we (simpply) could not fall backward. The

*rushing*        *simply*

wind was so strong that we could lean back against it and let it support us

as firmly as a brick wall would.

My brothers and I decided to take a short walk downwind along the

beach. We allowed the wind to push us along at a (rappid) pace. For a while

*rapid*

we (stoped) walking altogether. We simply jumped into the air, let ourselves

*stopped*

be blown along like empty milk (cartoons) and landed. Then we jumped into

*cartons*

the air again. (Borne) by the wind, we progressed as quickly as if we had

*Blown*

been walking.

# Make a Cause-and-Effect Chain

Write a series of causes and effects that tells a story about weather. Write each sentence on a strip below.

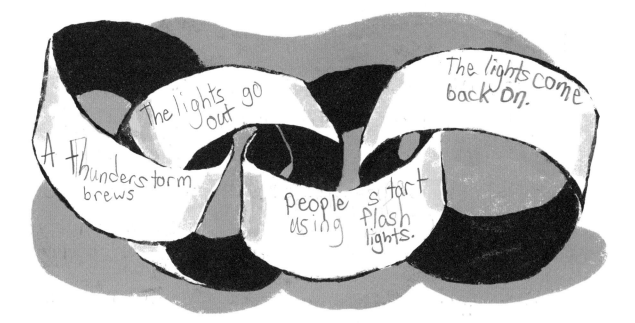

A Thunderstorm brews

The lights go out

People start using flash lights.

The lights come back on.

# Write a Letter

Write a letter describing a day in school. Include your feelings about the day's events. After you have revised your letter, proofread it. Show your letter to a friend.

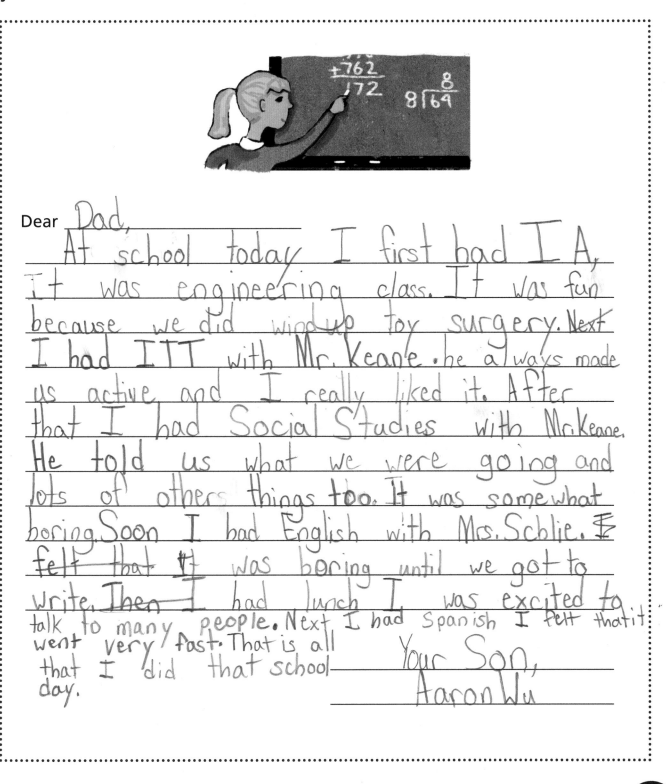

Dear Dad,

At school today I first had I A, It was engineering class. It was fun because we did wind up toy surgery. Next I had ITT with Mr. Keane. he always made us active and I really liked it. After that I had Social Studies with Mr. Keane. He told us what we were going and lots of others things too. It was somewhat boring. Soon I had English with Mrs. Schlie. I felt that it was boring until we got to write. Then I had lunch I was excited to talk to many people. Next I had Spanish I felt that it went very fast. That is all that I did that school day.

Your Son,
Aaron Wu

# Write a Lifeguard's Report

Imagine that you are a lifeguard. You have rescued a surfer who was dragged out to sea. Write a personal narrative of the rescue. Be sure your narrative has a beginning, a middle, and an end.

Today I rescued a surfer and I am going tell you all about it. At first it was a normal day when all of a sudden I heard this voice saying, "Help Me!" I searched with my binoculars until I found the person. At last there she was! As quickly as I could I dove into the water and put her in one hand. I was getting tired but I could not stop. We soon got to land and I first checked their airway. It was okay. Then I checked their breathing and it was okay. After that I checked their heart. It wasn't pumping! So I pushed hard on her chest and she revived. I would never forget the moment I rescued a surfer.

# Tell a Story about an Event in Your Life

Complete each of these sentences as a writing idea. Then, choose one writing idea and write a personal narrative on it.

The most exciting place I ever visited was

_Taiwain_

My most embarrassing moment was when

_I belly flopped_

The most unusual person I ever met was

_Kevin_

---

The most exciting place I ever went was Taiwain. It was exciting because we got to do so many things like going to night markets, playing games, eating, and visiting relatives. We also went to amazing places where there were plants, and other things. Taiwain will always be a place that I won't forget.

# A Practice Autobiographical Sketch

## JULY THE FOURTH ON THE LLANO RIVER

We have family reunions every July 4th. I can't remember any of them but one. It was last year when we met at the Llano River. That's when I learned to swim.

We arrived at my aunt's house on Friday night. My cousin J.W. was already there. J.W. is in high school. He is loud and funny and a real pain. Every summer, he finds one of us younger kids and picks on us the whole time we are together. That year, it was my turn.

It started as soon as he saw me. "Hey, kid," he asked, "did you ever learn to swim? Are you going to do that doggy paddle thing again this year?" I hung my head down, embarrassed in front of my other cousins. My embarrassment didn't seem to bother J.W. He kept right on poking fun. "You know, kid, you remind me a lot of Aunt Betty's cocker spaniel when you're in the water. Pant, splash, pant, splash. Don't get me wrong. I love it. It's a scream and probably makes you popular with all of your friends back home. That's how everyone swims there, right?" I slipped away as quietly as I could.

The next morning, all the kids went down to the river right after breakfast. I sat around with the grown-ups. I couldn't bring myself to go down to the river. I kept talking to myself, building up my courage. It took until lunchtime for me to find it.

I grabbed a towel from the bathroom closet, put on my flip-flops, and marched down to the river. I may have looked like a cocker spaniel, but who cared? It was just J.W. talking, and I didn't need his opinion. Most of my cousins were in the water, splashing, tubing, and diving for pennies.

The afternoon sun was warm and made the water feel great. I dragged one of the inner tubes on the bank into the water and plopped inside it. I wasn't afraid to float down the rapids in a tube. It was fun, and I stayed on the surface of the water, even when the rapids were fast.

As I floated near the rapids, I saw my cousin Danny. He's a little guy and always funny to watch. He was too small for the tube and sat low. When the water shot him across the rocks, Danny bumped all the way down the river. He always got out at the end of the rapids rubbing his backside. He didn't seem to mind, though. Danny was always the first one to run back up the riverbank to get ahead of the rapids and start again.

Just below the rapids, the river had carved a deep swimming hole. I pulled my tube out of the water and watched my cousins playing from the bank. I really wanted to be out there with them, but what was the point? There was J.W., splashing, laughing, and dunking the little kids under the water. No way was I going out there.

About the time I was getting ready to leave, Donnie, my brother, swam over to the bank. He sat with me in a shallow place near some large rocks. The water was really warm there. We talked about the river, about swimming, and about J.W. Then Donnie did something surprising. He leaned over and whispered in my ear, "If you want to learn to swim, I'll help you." The idea sounded great to me.

"Can you teach me now?" I asked excitedly. I remember that made Donnie laugh.

"Hold on there, little spaniel, let's get in deeper water first," he said as he smiled.

We walked over to an area that was not too deep. Donnie showed me how to hold my face in the water and turn it to the side to breathe. I wasn't crazy about putting my face in the water at first. I had to practice for a while, but Donnie didn't seem to mind.

Next, he showed me how to move my arms in a big circle. Then we put breathing and circling together. When I could do both things at the same time, I thought I was ready. I didn't know what was coming next.

We moved into deeper water. I could still feel the river bottom squishing between my toes. Donnie told me to float on my back. That was easy. Then he told me to turn over and float on my stomach. That was hard. All of a sudden, water rushed into my nose. I couldn't breathe and I panicked. I started imitating a cocker spaniel again, a frightened one. So Donnie pulled my head up and helped me stand. I couldn't stop coughing and spitting out water. I think I spit out a tadpole, but Donnie told me I was imagining things.

When I looked up along the bank, I saw my mom and dad watching me. At first, my mom looked worried, but then I saw her smile. Her smile made me determined. I told Donnie I was ready to try again. We stayed in the water so long that my fingers shriveled like old raisins. At first, I swam circles around Donnie. Then the circles got bigger and bigger. I knew how to swim!

When I was too tired to move anymore, I swam back to where Donnie sat on the bank. By the time I got there, all of my cousins were there, too. Even J.W. was there. He helped me out of the water, slapped me on the back, and said, "Hey, little spaniel, you're not a puppy anymore." That was J.W.'s idea of a compliment, and I was glad to take it.

# Respond to the Practice Paper

**Write your answers to the following questions or directions.**

1. In an autobiographical sketch, a writer talks about something important that happened to him or her. What important thing happened to this writer?

   _The important thing that happened to this writer is that he learned to swim._

2. How would you describe the setting for this story?

   _The setting of the story is in nature where there is a lake and a rapids._

3. What is the first clue the writer gives you to tell you what J.W. is like?

   _The first clue the writer gives me about J.W. is that he is a bully. because he picks on his younger cousins._

4. Based on the story, how would you describe the relationship between the writer and Donnie, his brother?

   _The relationship between the writer and Donnie is very close and can't be broken._

5. Write a paragraph to summarize the story. Think about the story's main ideas and what happens first, second, and so on. Also, think about how the story ends.

   _This story is about a boy who did not know how to swim. He was visiting his aunt's house with his cousins. One of his cousins J.W. picked on all of the younger cousins and it was the writer's turn. After a while his brother taught him how to swim and J.W. did not pick on him after that._

# Analyze the Practice Paper

Read "July the Fourth on the Llano River" again. As you read, think about how the writer wrote the story. Answer the following questions or directions.

1. How does the writer add emotion, or strong feeling, to this story?

   The writer adds emotion, by describing facial expressions, and using descriptive words like shriveled and old raisins.

2. Read the third paragraph again. Why do you think the writer used dialogue in this paragraph?

   The writer used dialogue in the third paragraph because it helps us understand his mood at that time and more about J.W.

3. How does the writer use humor to tell this story?

   The writer uses humor to tell this story by describing somethings in funny ways like when J.W. said that the writer looked like a cocker spaniel.

4. What does the writer do to help you "see" J.W. as he sees him?

   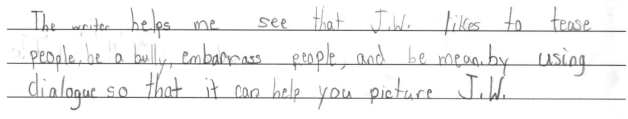

   The writer helps me see that J.W. likes to tease people, be a bully, embarrass people, and be mean by using dialogue so that it can help you picture J.W.

# Writing Assignment

Write an autobiographical sketch about something important that happened to you. Write about something you remember well. Use this writing plan to help you write a first draft on the next page.

**What important thing happened to you?**

An important thing that happened to me was when I got all As except 1 B

▼

**What happened first? How will you describe it?**

I first got my report card. I was really hoping I got all straight As.

▼

**What happened second? How will you describe it?**

I went home and I could not wait

▼

**What happened last? How will you describe it?**

I opened it and I did my best and I got 1 "B" and "I" all A's.

# First Draft

TIPS FOR WRITING AN AUTOBIOGRAPHICAL SKETCH:

- Write about something important that happened to you.
- Write about something you remember well.
- Give details that help explain your experience.
- Describe events in the order that they happened.

Use your writing plan as a guide for writing your first draft of an autobiographical sketch. Include a catchy title.

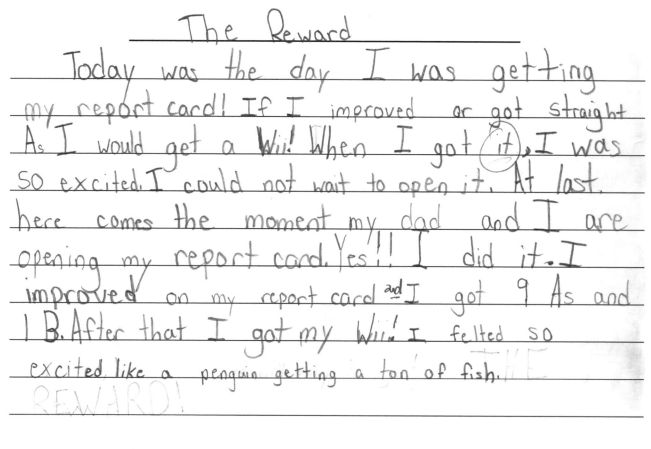

The Reward

Today was the day I was getting my report card! If I improved or got straight As I would get a Wii! When I got it, I was so excited. I could not wait to open it. At last, here comes the moment my dad and I are opening my report card. Yes!! I did it. I improved on my report card and I got 9 As and 1 B. After that I got my Wii! I felted so excited like a penguin getting a ton of fish. THE REWARD!

(Continue on your own paper.)

# Revise the Draft

Use the chart below to help you revise your draft. Check YES or NO to answer each question in the chart. If you answer NO, make notes to remind yourself how you can revise, or change, your writing to improve it.

| Question | YES ✔ | NO ✔ | If the answer is NO, what will you do to improve your writing? |
|---|---|---|---|
| Does your autobiographical sketch describe something important that happened to you? | ✓ | | |
| Does your story have a clear setting? | ✓ | ✓ | I could say I was at school and home. |
| Do you include important characters in your story? | ✓ | | |
| Do you use specific details to help you tell your story? | ✓ | | |
| Do you describe events in the order they happened? | ✓ | | |
| Have you corrected mistakes in spelling, grammar, and punctuation? | ✓ | | |

Use the notes in your chart and your writing plan to revise your draft.

# Writing Report Card

Read your revised draft again or ask someone else to read it. Have the person who reads your paper complete the following Report Card. Revise your paper until you have no less than a Very Good Score for each item.

Title of paper: _____

Purpose of paper: _*This paper is an autobiographical sketch. It describes*_

_*something important that happened in my life.*_

Person who scores the paper: _____

| Score | Writing Goals |
|---|---|
| | Is this story an example of an autobiographical sketch? |
| | Is the setting described in detail? |
| | Does the writer use important characters to help tell the story? |
| | Does the writer describe specific events? |
| | Does the writer use important details to help explain events? |
| | Does the writer describe events in the order they happen? |
| | Does the writer convince you that this experience was important to him or her? |
| | Are the story's grammar, spelling, and punctuation correct? |

☺ Excellent Score  ☆ Very Good Score  + Good Score
✔ Acceptable Score  − Needs Improvement

# UNIT 2: How-to Writing

## HOW MUCH DO YOU KNOW?

Use the following sentences to write a how-to paragraph. First, write the topic sentence that gives the purpose of the instructions. Then write the steps in correct time order. Finally, answer the question that follows.

- Finally, casually drop the ball of tuna on the floor.
- First, make a small ball of tuna around the pill.
- You will need the pill, a can of tuna, and a plate.
- It's often not easy to give a dog a pill, but with the help of a little tuna fish, it can be done.
- The dog will eat the tuna and never realize the pill was inside!
- Next, put the tuna ball on a plate.
- Sit at the kitchen table and pretend to eat the tuna ball.

You will need the pill, or can of tuna, and a plate. It's often not easy to give a dog a pill, but with the help of a little tuna fish, it can be done. First, make a small ball of tuna around the pill. Next, put the tuna ball on a plate. Sit at the kitchen table and pretend to eat the tuna ball. Finally, casually drop the ball of tuna on the floor. The dog will eat the tuna and never realize the pill was inside!

What materials were needed in the instructions above?

You need the pill, a can of tuna, and a plate.

# Analyzing a How-to Paragraph

A HOW-TO PARAGRAPH

- tells how to do something
- has a topic sentence and detail sentences
- tells what materials to use and what steps to follow

Use the following sentences to write a how-to paragraph. First, write the topic sentence that gives the purpose of the instructions. Next, write the sentence that lists the needed materials. Then write the steps in correct time order. Put in any special information where it is needed.

[7]Boil the ginger, letting the water evaporate until only one cup of water remains.[2] You will need a fresh ginger root, three cups of water, a knife, and a glass pot or kettle.[1]If you ever need to warm your body when you are chilled, you should try making some ginger tea.[3]First, put three cups of water into the glass pot.[4]Next, cut six slices of ginger root. [5]The slices should be $\frac{1}{8}$- to $\frac{1}{4}$-inch thick.[8]Strain the ginger tea into a cup.[9]Drink it hot.[6]Add the ginger to the water in the pot.

> If you ever need to warm your body when you are chilled, you should try making some ginger tea. You will need a fresh ginger root, three cups of water, a knife, and a glass pot or kettle. First, put three cups of water into the glass pot. Next, cut six slices of ginger root. The slices should be $\frac{1}{8}$-to$\frac{1}{4}$-inch thick. Add the ginger to the water in the pot. Boil the ginger, letting the water evaporate until only one cup of water remains. Strain the ginger tea into a cup. Drink it hot.

# Visualizing Steps in a Process

Read the following instructions. Answer the questions that follow.

**Fooling Your Friends with Dishwater Punch**

An April Fool's Day party can be fun. You can fool and surprise your friends by serving them this delicious punch. It looks like dishwater. Do not let your friends see you make the punch. You will need the following items:

- a bowl that holds at least three quarts

- a package of green drink mix

- one quart of orange juice

- one quart of lemon soda

- one pint of pineapple sherbet

- a large spoon

First, pour the orange juice into the bowl. Next, add the package of green drink mix. Stir it in. The juice should look grayish, like dishwater. Add the sherbet in small scoops. Stir the mixture briskly with a spoon until some of the sherbet is melted. Then, add the lemon soda. The punch should look like soapy dishwater.

Offer the punch to your friends and tell them it is dishwater. If none of them will try it, drink a glass yourself. When someone finally tries it, shout "April Fool!"

**What steps might the writer of these directions have gone through before writing? Complete the chart below with notes the writer might have made while visualizing the steps. Include the steps in the right order, mentioning all the materials needed.**

| MATERIALS | STEPS |
|---|---|
| orange juice, bowl | 1. First, pour the orange juice into the bowl. |
| green drink mix, spoon | 2. Next, add the package of green drink mix and stir. |
| pineapple sherbet | 3. Then add the pineapple sherbert in small scoops. |
| spoon | 4. Stir the mixture briskly with a spoon until some of the sherbert melts. |
| lemon soda | 5. Then, add the lemon soda. |

# Adjusting for Audience and Purpose

Good writers adjust their writing for their audience and purpose.

Read the pair of how-to paragraphs below. Decide whether each paragraph has been written for a second-grader or for a sixth-grader. Circle your answer. Then write a sentence on the lines that gives at least two reasons for your answers.

A. Send secret messages to your friends! You will need a white crayon, white paper, and watery paint. First, write the message with the white crayon. Next, give the message to your friend. Say that you will do a little "magic." Paint over the message, and it will appear.

(for a second-grader)          for a sixth-grader

B. Write a secret message! You will need a white crayon, white paper, and watery paint. First, write the message on the white paper. Use the white crayon. Next, give the message to your friend. Say that you will do a little "magic." Paint over the message, and it will appear! The paint will not stick to the wax in the crayon. That is why you can see the message when you paint over it.

for a second-grader          (for a sixth-grader)

One reason why paragraph A. is for a second-grader because it is less specific and it does not have as much detail as the second paragraph. The second paragraph is for a sixth-grader because it would be confusing for a second-grader and it has a little extra at the end which a second-grader would not know what it means.

# Avoiding Wordy Language

> Good writers revise their compositions to avoid wordy language.

Rewrite each sentence of this recipe to make it more concise.

1. If you are very thirsty on a hot day, you can make a refreshing yogurt shake to drink.

   _On a hot day you can make a refreshing yogurt shake to drink._

2. First, you get an eight-ounce carton of plain yogurt and measure two tablespoons of plain yogurt into a blender.

   _Get an eight-ounce carton of plain yogurt and measure two tablespoons of yogurt into a blender._

3. Next, you can add two tablespoons of apple juice, orange juice, pineapple juice, or your favorite fruit juice.

   _You can add two tablespoons of apple, orange, pineapple, or your favorite fruit juice._

4. Get a jar of honey and take one-half teaspoon of the honey and add it.

   _Take one-half teaspoon of honey and add it._

5. Take a banana and cut off one-third of it and add it.

   _Cut off one-third of a banana and add it._

6. Find some nutmeg and add a pinch of it to the other ingredients.

   _Add a pinch of nutmeg with the other ingredients._

7. Take two ice cubes and crush them and then add them to the mixture.

   _Crush two ice cubes and then add them to the mixture._

8. Turn on the blender and blend the ingredients until they are frothy.

   _Blend the ingredients until they are frothy in the blender._

# Proofreading a How-to Paragraph

Proofread the beginning of the how-to paragraph below, paying special attention to commas. Use the Proofreading Marks to correct at least eight errors.

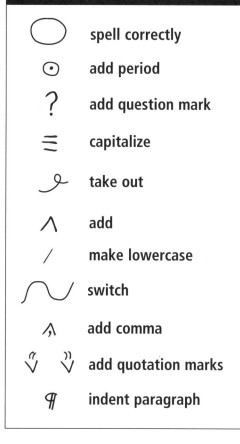

**PROOFREADING MARKS**

| | |
|---|---|
| ⬭ | spell correctly |
| ⊙ | add period |
| ? | add question mark |
| ≡ | capitalize |
| ℘ | take out |
| ∧ | add |
| / | make lowercase |
| ∿ | switch |
| ⋏ | add comma |
| ⌄⌄ | add quotation marks |
| ¶ | indent paragraph |

With the help of a little tuna fish and some acting skill, you can easily get your dog Titan to take his pill. As you know, Titan often begs for tuna but you never give him any. If you suddenly offer Titan some tuna with the pill inside it, he will become suspicious and refuse eat it. Try this method instead.

Make a small ball of tuna around Titan's pill. Put the tuna ball on a plate. Then find sumthing you like to eat and put that on the plate too. Take your plate and sit down at the kitchen table.

Titan will probably be watching you carefully but you should ignore him. He's a very smart dog and it will not be easy to fool him. your chances of success are best if you if just pretend you don't see him.

Titan will soon sit beside you, and start to beg. Eat your own food and continue to ignore Titan. Then, very casually, allow the ball of tuna to fall to the floor. You should make a quick grab for the tuna but you must be sure that Titan gets to it first. Titan will eagerly gulp the tuna–and the pill.

# List Steps in a Process

With a friend, choose a recipe for a favorite snack. Visualize the steps for preparing the snack and list them. One person might want to illustrate each step. Share your recipes.

| Materials | Steps | Illustrations |
|---|---|---|
|  | 1. |  |
|  | 2. |  |
|  | 3. |  |
|  | 4. |  |
|  | 5. |  |
|  | 6. |  |

# Write a Magazine Article

Pretend you are a writer for a gardening magazine. Work with a friend or two to plan and write a how-to paragraph on gardening. Revise and proofread your work.

_____

_____

_____

_____

_____

_____

_____

_____

_____

_____

_____

_____

_____

_____

# Making a Gift

Have you ever thought about making a gift for someone for a special holiday or birthday? Add two gift ideas to the list below. Then, choose one gift from the list and write a how-to paragraph on making one of these gifts.

picture frame

placemats

necklace

jewelry box

plant hanger

pencil holder

_____

_____

HOW TO MAKE _____

_____

_____

_____

_____

_____

_____

_____

# Explain What You Are Doing

Check whether you have ever been in one or more of the situations described below. Add one other situation like these. Then, choose one and write a how-to paragraph explaining your answer to a family member, friend, or classmate.

|  | YES | NO |
|---|---|---|
| 1. You are working on something in the garage, and a younger brother or sister asks, "What are you doing?" | ❏ | ❏ |
| 2. You are playing a computer game, and a friend asks, "How do you play that game?" | ❏ | ❏ |
| 3. You are working on a word problem for math, and a classmate asks, "How do you do those problems?" | ❏ | ❏ |

4. _____

_____

_____

_____

_____

# A Practice How-to Paper

## BUILD A NEWTON'S CRADLE

Sir Isaac Newton was an English mathematician and scientist who lived in the 1600s and 1700s. He published his three laws of motion, which describe how forces affect the motion of an object, in 1687. You can demonstrate one of Newton's laws of motion with an apparatus called a Newton's cradle. The cradle will show that things at rest tend to stay at rest until acted on by an outside force. A Newton's cradle also demonstrates what scientists call the "Principle of Conservation of Energy." That means that energy is never created or destroyed. Energy can change from one form to another, but the total amount of energy stays the same.

It is easier to understand these scientific principles if you use your own Newton's cradle. You need only a few materials to build one. They are:

- 1 ruler marked in inches
- 1 pencil or dowel rod
- 5 eight-inch pieces of fishing line
- 5 paper clips
- scissors
- 5 wooden beads

Once you have your materials, you are ready to begin building. Here's how:

First, use your ruler to make five marks on the pencil or dowel rod. The marks should be exactly one inch apart. Be sure the third mark is in the center of the pencil or dowel rod.

Second, use the scissors to score, or cut, a ring around each mark on the pencil or dowel rod. The ring should go all the way around the pencil or rod. Handle the scissors carefully so that you don't cut your skin.

Next, tie a paper clip to one end of each piece of fishing line. Place each paper clip in exactly the same place on each line.

Then, thread one piece of fishing line through the hole in each bead. Each bead will rest on a paper clip.

Now, tie each piece of fishing line around the scored rings on the pencil or dowel rod. The beads must line up exactly and hang evenly.

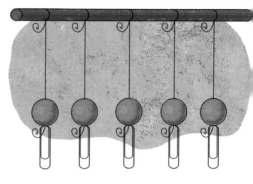

Use one hand to hold the pencil or rod horizontally. Pull the first bead on one end back. Then release it gently. Observe what happens. The bead you release exerts a force on the other beads.

Now consider the Principle of Conservation of Energy to examine what happens to the beads on your Newton's cradle. Before you released the bead, the bead had one kind of energy, called potential energy. When you let the bead fall, the potential energy changed into another kind of energy, called kinetic energy. Kinetic energy is the energy of motion.

Wait. There are still more changes in energy. When the first bead hit the second bead, what did you hear? You heard a click. A click is sound energy. Now think about what happens when two things rub together. For example, if you rub your hands together, can you feel your hands getting warmer? The kinetic energy in your hands changes to heat energy. The same thing happens with the beads on your Newton's cradle. As the first bead hits the second bead, energy moves through the beads to the bead at the other end. The bead lifts, swings back, and hits the line of beads. Each time a bead hits another bead, kinetic energy changes to sound and heat energy. Eventually, the kinetic energy changes completely to sound and heat, and the beads stop moving. But don't expect this to happen quickly. The changes of energy are small, so it takes some time for the beads to stop moving.

Now you know how to build a Newton's cradle. You also know how to use the cradle to demonstrate some interesting scientific principles. Try making other Newton's cradles. Use different sizes of dowel rods and string. Change the number of beads, or use metal beads. You might even want to demonstrate your super science skills for your class.

# Respond to the Practice Paper

**Write your answers to the following questions or directions.**

1. What materials do you need to make a Newton's cradle?

   _____

   _____

2. Why is it important that the beads line up exactly and evenly?

   _____

   _____

3. Why do you need fishing line?

   _____

   _____

4. In the last paragraph, the writer suggests that you build different kinds of Newton's cradles. Write a paragraph to describe the materials you would use if you could build any kind of Newton's cradle you wanted. Draw a picture to go with your paragraph.

   _____

   _____

   _____

# Analyze the Practice Paper

Read "Build a Newton's Cradle" again. As you read, think about why the writer wrote this paper. What did the writer do to help explain how to build a cradle? Write your answers to the following questions or directions.

1. Name at least two things that make this paper a good example of a how-to paper.

   _____

   _____

2. Read the first paragraph again. Why do you think the writer included this paragraph in a how-to paper?

   _____

   _____

3. Why does the writer list the materials you need to make a cradle before telling you how to do it?

   _____

   _____

4. Why does the writer use words like *first*, *next*, and *then*?

   _____

   _____

5. Read the next-to-the-last paragraph on page 40 again. Draw pictures to go with the words the writer uses to explain the Principle of Conservation of Energy.

# Writing Assignment

Think about something you want to tell others how to do. Use this writing plan to help you write a first draft on the next page.

**What will you tell others how to do?**

▼

**List the materials someone will need.**

▼

**Write the steps someone should follow in order. Number the steps.**

▼

**Write some sequence words that help the reader know what to do.**

# First Draft

TIPS FOR WRITING A HOW-TO PAPER:

- Choose one thing to teach someone.
- Focus on a plan.
  1. Think of all the materials someone will need.
  2. Think of all the steps someone will follow.
- Use sequence words in your directions.

Use your writing plan as a guide as you write your first draft of a how-to paper. Include a catchy title.

_____

_____

_____

_____

_____

_____

_____

_____

_____

_____

_____

(Continue on your own paper.)

# Revise the Draft

Use the chart below to help you revise your draft. Check YES or NO to answer each question in the chart. If you answer NO, make notes to remind yourself how you can revise, or change, your writing to improve it.

| Question | YES ✓ | NO ✓ | If the answer is NO, what will you do to improve your writing? |
|---|---|---|---|
| Does your paper teach someone how to do something? | | | |
| Do you use the first paragraph to introduce the project or task? | | | |
| Do you include all of the materials someone needs? | | | |
| Do you explain all of the steps someone must follow? | | | |
| Are the steps in order? | | | |
| Do you explain each step clearly so that it is easy to follow? | | | |
| Do you use sequence words to help guide your reader? | | | |
| Have you corrected mistakes in spelling, grammar, and punctuation? | | | |

Use the notes in your chart and your writing plan to revise your draft.

# Writing Report Card

Read your revised draft again or ask someone else to read it. Have the person who reads your paper complete the following Report Card. Revise your paper until you have no less than a Very Good Score for each item.

Title of paper: _____

Purpose of paper: _This paper explains how to do something._____

Person who scores the paper: _____

| Score | Writing Goals |
|---|---|
| | Does the writer introduce the topic in the first paragraph? |
| | Does the paper teach someone how to do something? |
| | Does the paper include the materials that someone needs? |
| | Does the paper explain each step that someone will follow? |
| | Are the steps in order? |
| | Is each step written clearly to make it easy to follow? |
| | Are there sequence words to help the reader understand? |
| | Are the paper's grammar, spelling, and punctuation correct? |

☺ Excellent Score   ☆ Very Good Score   + Good Score
✔ Acceptable Score   − Needs Improvement

# UNIT 3: Descriptive Writing

## HOW MUCH DO YOU KNOW?

Read the paragraph. Underline the topic sentence. Then fill in the chart below. List the details that the writer used to appeal to each sense. Write *none* if there are none.

<u>Each summer Ron and Diane go to their favorite vacation spot—their great-aunt's beach house.</u> The three-bedroom house has a view of the ocean in the front and a mountain range in the back.

As soon as they arrived this year, everyone headed out for a walk on the beach. The cuckoo clock sounded just before they left. They had two hours to explore before dinner. Piles of slippery seaweed had washed up on the sand. Ron noticed a jellyfish on one of the piles. Unfortunately, it smelled liked dead fish. They heard the bark of a sea lion in the distance. Looking out across the blue-green water, Diane spotted the sea lion on a distant rock.

As the shadows of the palm trees lengthened, the beachfront grew quiet. Soon, their walk would draw to a close. Diane picked up a large, smooth shell. They turned toward the house singing "The Twelve Days of Christmas" even though it was July.

| sight | The shadows of the palm trees lengthened. Jelly-fish. blue-green water. |
| --- | --- |
| hearing | House singing Barking of the sealion |
| smell | Dead fish |
| taste | None |
| touch | The piles of slippery seaweed |

# Analyzing a Descriptive Paragraph

> **A DESCRIPTIVE PARAGRAPH**
> - creates a picture with words
> - presents sensory details in a clear order
> - has a topic sentence and detail sentences

**Read the paragraph. Underline the topic sentence. Then complete the items below.**

The room had clearly been ransacked. The drawers of the dresser next to the window were open and empty. A trail of assorted clothing led to the closet. The closet stood empty, its contents strewn across the bed and the floor. Glass from a broken perfume bottle crunched loudly underfoot, the fragrance of its contents mixing with the smell of garlic. The only item left undisturbed was a portrait on the wall over the bed. Its subject, a solemn young woman, stared thoughtfully into the room, like a silent witness to the recent crime.

1. List at least five words or phrases the writer used to appeal to your senses. After each word or phrase, tell which sense it is: *sight, hearing, smell, taste,* or *touch.*

   The fragrance of the broken perfume bottle mixed with garlic.
   That is the sense of smell. The glass of a broken perfume
   bottle crunched loudly. That is the sense of hearing.

2. Is this paragraph written in space order or in time order? What words did the writer use that indicate this type of order?

   A trail of assorted clothing led to the closet. That is the sense
   of sight. There is no sense of taste or touch.

# Observing Details

> **TO WRITE A DESCRIPTIVE PARAGRAPH, GOOD WRITERS**
> - include specific details
> - arrange details in the way that makes the most sense for their purpose
> - use words that appeal to the reader's senses

**Read the following paragraphs. Then fill in the chart below. List the details that the writer used to appeal to each sense.**

After swimming for about a hundred yards, Marlene stopped and looked back at the island. From the top of the volcano, lush green vegetation grew down to meet the soft white sands of the beach. The white sands disappeared into the shimmering blue of the ocean.

Marlene rested for a moment. She enjoyed the contrast of the cool water on her body and the hot sun on her face. It was quiet except for the sound of the surf thundering on the shore.

Marlene tasted the salty water on her lips and thought about the luau that would begin very soon. The smoky smell of the roasting pig drifted out and mixed with the salty smells of the ocean. Marlene heard her stomach growl and began to swim to shore.

| | |
|---|---|
| sight | vegetation grew, island, white sands, shimmering blue of the ocean |
| hearing | stomach growling, the surf thundering onto the shore. |
| smell | salty smells, smokey smell of roasting pig. |
| taste | salty water, |
| touch | cool water, |

# Using Precise Words

> Good writers use precise words to create
> clear pictures for the reader.

Read each pair of sentences. Underline the sentence that is imprecise, or general. Then rewrite the sentence. Use precise words to create a clearer picture.

1. Bob heard a noise at the door.
   He could barely hear it over the wail of the siren outside.

   _____

2. Bob stood up quickly.
   He moved to the front door.

   _____

3. A person was there.
   A girl was beside him.

   _____

4. Sorrow was written all over the boy's face.
   The girl seemed unhappy.

   _____

5. "Have you seen any strange cats around?" asked the boy.
   "We have lost our tabby."

   _____

6. "Does your cat have spots?" asked Bob.
   "Yes, he also has black patches," answered the girl.

   _____

7. "I found him on the chair in my backyard," said Bob.
   "He is sleeping."

   _____

# Expanding Sentences

Good writers add details as they revise, so their descriptions paint complete word pictures.

Expand each sentence with descriptive details. Follow the instructions in parentheses ( ) to rewrite each sentence.

1. A dog huddled in the shelter of the tunnel. (Add details about the subject.)

   _____

   _____

2. It shivered in the wind. (Add descriptive details about an item in the complete predicate.)

   _____

3. Finally, it left the shelter of the tunnel. (Add another predicate.)

   _____

   _____

4. Its shadow trailed behind it. (Add descriptive details about the subject.)

   _____

5. The dog trotted down the street. (Add another subject.)

   _____

6. The dog broke through the sheet of ice on the puddle. (Add descriptive details about an item in the complete predicate, and add a second predicate.)

   _____

   _____

# Proofreading a Descriptive Paragraph

## PROOFREADING HINT

To be a good proofreader, look for one type of error at a time. For example, proofread once for capitalization errors, once for punctuation errors, and once for spelling errors.

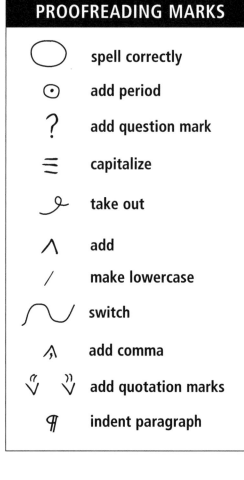

### PROOFREADING MARKS

- ◯     spell correctly
- ⊙     add period
- ?     add question mark
- ≡     capitalize
- ℘     take out
- ∧     add
- /     make lowercase
- ∿     switch
- ∧     add comma
- ⌄ ⌄     add quotation marks
- ¶     indent paragraph

Proofread the description, paying special attention to the capitalization and the end punctuation of sentences. Use the Proofreading Marks to correct at least eight errors.

A set of smooth stone steps led up to a flat clearing in the forest Here the sun's rays filtered down through the branches of the towering pines, and the ground was covered with fragrant green pine needles. the carpet of needles felt thick and soft under Nina's feet.

a gentle breeze rustled the branches Nina inhaled the scent of the

pines as it drifted on the breeze. mingled with the scent of pine was the smell of the pale green mosses growing on the north sides of the trees.

What was that in the middle of the clearing Nina saw a large stump, just under three feat tall and a full three feet in diameter. four smaller stumps were arranged around it Paul was already seated on one of the smaller stumps, and the large stump was clearly just the right hieght for a table.

On the large stump lay a basket of juicy blackberries, a canteen, and two shiny metal cups Paul looked up at Nina and asked, "Are you ready for a treat?"

# Observe and Write Details

Work with a friend. In a book or a magazine, find a picture of a place you both would like to visit. Study the picture for a few minutes. Write the name of the place and some interesting details about it. Then write a descriptive paragraph about the place.

## WE WOULD LIKE TO VISIT

_____

_____

_____

_____

# Write a Visitor's Guide

Working with a friend or two, list places that visitors might like to visit in your community. Then, choose one place from the list and write a descriptive paragraph about that place.

_____

_____

_____

_____

_____

_____

_____

_____

_____

_____

_____

_____

# Write an Action Paragraph

Find an action photograph in the sports section of a newspaper or magazine. Cut out the photograph and glue it to this page. Write a descriptive paragraph about the photograph. Be sure to use strong action verbs. Revise and proofread your work.

# Rediscover Familiar Buildings

Have you ever looked closely at a familiar building? Use the following checklist to rediscover buildings in your area. You may add other buildings to the checklist. Choose one building from the list and write a descriptive paragraph about the building.

| building | pillars | arches | tower | window | balcony | courtyard | stairway |
|----------|---------|--------|-------|--------|---------|-----------|----------|
| school   |         |        |       |        |         |           |          |
| hotel    |         |        |       |        |         |           |          |
| pharmacy |         |        |       |        |         |           |          |
| barn     |         |        |       |        |         |           |          |
|          |         |        |       |        |         |           |          |
|          |         |        |       |        |         |           |          |

_____

_____

_____

_____

_____

_____

_____

# A Practice Descriptive Story

## WEEKEND FRIENDS

Cole's dad was unusually late picking him up on Friday night. Cole didn't say anything to his mother, but he was a little worried. His dad was never late. Cole sat quietly, tracing the stitching in his overnight bag. Finally, the phone rang. Cole's mom rushed to the kitchen to answer it. "He's on his way," she announced with relief. "He got tied up at the office."

Soon Cole and his dad were in the car driving to his dad's apartment. "Sorry about that, Cole," his dad said. "Something came up at the office. I know it's too late to do much tonight. But," he added, "I have a special day planned tomorrow. I hope you don't mind."

"It's okay, Dad," Cole said quickly. Cole knew that their weekends together were as important to his dad as they were to him.

The next morning, golden rays spilled through Cole's bedroom window. Saturday had come. By the time his dad got up, Cole was already dressed and eating breakfast. "Wow," his dad said. "You're in a hurry this morning." His dad smiled. "Let me finish this cup of coffee, and we'll be on our way, okay?" Cole nodded.

The highway was a gray stripe through green countryside. On either side, wildflowers bounced in the wind. Their red and yellow heads moved up and down like fishing bobs on a lake. Cole's dad slowed the car and turned right onto a farm road. Then he turned again, this time onto a dirt road that sliced the pasture.

Cole's dad stopped the car. "Well, what do you think?" Cole looked puzzled. "What do you mean?" he asked.

His dad laughed softly. "This is our farm. This is why I was late last night. I had to sign the papers." Cole looked amazed. His eyes widened and his mouth fell open, but he couldn't speak a word.

Cole and his dad walked through the pasture to a row of graceful trees. The deep green live oaks and the giant cottonwoods bowed over a narrow creek. The creek babbled like a child. The sun's rays sparkled on the water. Cole and his dad sat on the bank. "What do you think, Cole?"

Cole turned slowly, forcing his eyes away from the creek. "I love it," he almost whispered.

His dad took him toward the old farmhouse beyond the creek. "I thought we could come here on the weekends, Cole. We could fix up the house together. I could use the help. Wait until you see it. It's been empty for more than forty years."

"Who lived here then, Dad?" Cole asked.

"I don't know," said his dad. "The agent said the last owner never used the house. He just let it fall down. He's the person who sold the farm."

They reached the farmhouse and, for the second time in one day, Cole didn't know what to say. This was the tallest, oldest, most run-down house he'd ever seen. He loved it. "Wow!" Cole yelled. "Cool house! This is great!" Cole started running.

His dad yelled, "Cole, slow down. You can't trust those steps. Wait." But Cole couldn't hear the last warning. It came just as his leg went through a rotten step. The bottom half of his body disappeared, swallowed by the steps. Cole's dad raced over. "Are you okay, Cole? Can you move?" he asked, with panic in his voice.

Cole groaned a little as his dad pulled him from the step. "I'm fine, really. I don't think anything's broken." While his dad checked his legs, Cole lay on the porch. His head turned toward the jagged hole. "Dad, I think there's something in there. Look." His dad ignored him and continued to ask what hurt.

"Dad, what is it?" Cole asked. He'd forgotten about his legs.

Cole's dad looked inside the hole. "I don't know, Cole, but you stay here. I'll go in this time." He squeezed through the hole, landing with a thud. When he came back up, he had a box caked in decades of dirt. He and Cole used a pocketknife to remove the dirt and pick the small, rusting lock that kept the box sealed.

"Wow," they said at the same time. Inside were a small leather box and a dirty envelope. The box contained a World War II Medal of Honor. Even now, the eagle shined and the ribbon looked fresh. Inside the envelope was a certificate and a single photograph. "Horace Mickel," Cole's dad said, reading the name on the certificate. "I'd say this medal and this house must have belonged to him."

"Who was Horace Mickel, Dad? Do you think he left anything else under those steps?" Cole asked. "Or in the house?" he added eagerly.

"I don't know," his dad chuckled. "Let's forget the steps for now. If you think you can get yourself up, we'll start looking for the answers to your questions inside." Cole's dad unlocked the front door and held Cole's elbow as Cole hobbled inside. The wind came with them, disturbing dust that had sat comfortably for forty years. Spider webs as fine as lace capped their heads.

"This is great, Dad. It looks like Mr. Mickel left everything behind. There are bound to be clues everywhere."

"I think you're right, Cole. But I have an idea. Let's not try to find all of our answers today. Let's make this last awhile. Let's make this our weekend project, and we'll come to know Mr. Mickel a little at a time, just like friends normally do." His dad hugged him hard.

"Good idea, Dad. I think I'll put this photograph above the fireplace. Then we'll know where to find Mr. Mickel when we come back."

# Respond to the Practice Paper

**Write your answers to the following questions or directions.**

1. What makes this story an example of descriptive writing?

   _____

   _____

2. How does the writer let you know that Cole and his mom are nervous?

   _____

   _____

3. How does the writer let you know that Cole loves his dad, the farm, and the farmhouse?

   _____

   _____

4. Use a separate piece of paper to draw a picture of your favorite description in this story. Label your picture.

5. Write a paragraph to summarize the story. Use these questions to help you write your summary:
   • What are the main ideas of the story?
   • What happens first? Second? Third?
   • How does the story end?

   _____

   _____

   _____

   _____

   _____

   _____

# Analyze the Practice Paper

Read "Weekend Friends" again. As you read, think about how the writer achieved his or her purpose for writing. Write your answers to the following questions or directions.

1. Read the fifth and eighth paragraphs again. What similes does the writer use? (A simile uses the word *like* or *as* to compare two things.)

   _____

   _____

2. What metaphor does the writer use in the fifth paragraph? (A metaphor does not use the word *like* or *as* to compare two things.)

   _____

   _____

3. List some interesting verbs the writer uses to describe the action in paragraphs 5, 8, 14, and 15.

   _____

   _____

4. Use a separate piece of paper to draw a picture of the description in paragraph 20.

5. Write a paragraph to describe what the farmhouse will look like when Cole and his dad finish fixing it up.

   _____

   _____

   _____

   _____

   _____

   _____

   _____

# Writing Assignment

To describe something, a writer tells what he or she sees, hears, feels, tastes, and smells. The writer uses interesting words. The writer also compares things to other things, like a creek to a babbling child. Describe something that you and a relative or friend did together. Use this writing plan to help you write a first draft on the next page.

**What experience would you like to describe? Write it in the circle. Then write words, similes, or metaphors that describe the experience on the lines.**

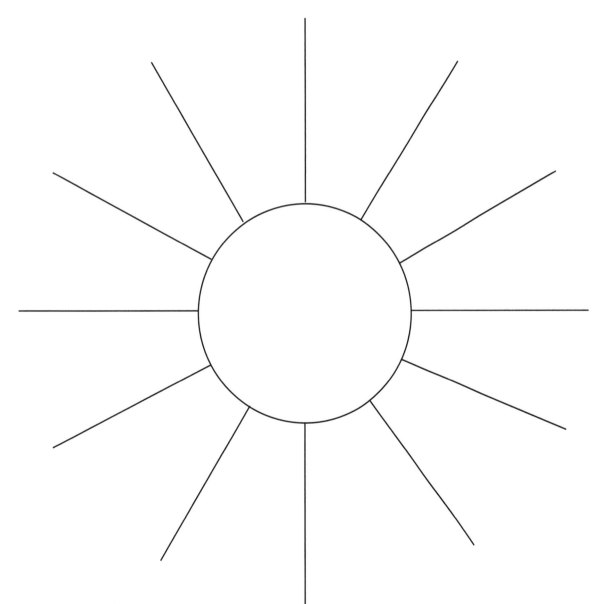

# First Draft

TIPS FOR WRITING A DESCRIPTIVE STORY:

- Use your voice when you write. That means you should use your special way of expressing yourself.

- Help readers see, smell, taste, feel, and hear what you are writing about.

- Use interesting words to help you describe.

- Use similes and metaphors to help your readers imagine the experience you are writing about.

Use your writing plan as a guide as you write your first draft of a descriptive story. Include a catchy title.

_____

_____

_____

_____

_____

_____

_____

_____

(Continue on your own paper.)

# Revise the Draft

Use the chart below to help you revise your draft. Check YES or NO to answer each question in the chart. If you answer NO, make notes to remind yourself how you can revise, or change, your writing to improve it.

| Question | YES ✔ | NO ✔ | If the answer is NO, what will you do to improve your writing? |
|---|---|---|---|
| Do you describe something that happened to you and a relative or friend? | | | |
| Do you describe what you see, hear, smell, taste, and feel? | | | |
| Do you use action words to describe what happens? | | | |
| Do you use descriptive similes and metaphors? | | | |
| Do you describe events in the order they happen? | | | |
| Have you corrected mistakes in spelling, grammar, and punctuation? | | | |

Use the notes in your chart and your writing plan to revise your draft.

# Writing Report Card

Read your revised draft again or ask someone else to read it. Have the person who reads your paper complete the following Report Card. Revise your paper until you have no less than a Very Good Score for each item.

Title of paper: _____

Purpose of paper: __*This paper is a descriptive story. It describes*__

__*something a friend or relative and I did together.*__

Person who scores the paper: _____

| Score | Writing Goals |
|---|---|
|  | Does this story tell about something that happened to the writer and a friend or relative? |
|  | Are the events that happen in the story in order? |
|  | Does the writer describe what he or she sees, hears, tastes, smells, and feels? |
|  | Does the writer use interesting action words? |
|  | Does the story include descriptive similes and metaphors? |
|  | Are the story's grammar, spelling, and punctuation correct? |

☺ Excellent Score    ☆ Very Good Score    + Good Score

✔ Acceptable Score    − Needs Improvement

# UNIT 4: Comparative Writing

## HOW MUCH DO YOU KNOW?

**A. Read each paragraph. Label it** *comparison* **or** *contrast.*

My friends Lena and Taylor are alike in many ways. Both are intelligent, loyal, and helpful. Either can carry on a great conversation. Each has an excellent sense of humor, and they enjoy many of the same activities.

1. _____

My two friends Lena and Taylor are different in many ways. Lena complains if she does not like something, and she argues if she disagrees with me. Taylor rarely complains or argues, so we almost never fight. But, Lena is a more honest friend. She says exactly what she thinks or feels. In contrast, Taylor never says anything negative to me about things I have said or done. Instead, she may say something to someone else, and her comments often get back to me.

2. _____

**B. Use the paragraphs to answer the questions below.**

3. In what one way are the two friends alike?

_____

_____

4. In what one way are the two friends different?

_____

_____

# Analyzing Paragraphs of Comparison and Contrast

A PARAGRAPH OF COMPARISON OR CONTRAST
- tells about the similarities or the differences of two or more items
- answers the same questions about each item

Read each paragraph. Label it *comparison* or *contrast*. Circle the names of the two items being compared. Underline the key words that signal similarity or difference.

1. The new house was similar to the old house in some ways. Like the old house, it had three bedrooms. Both houses had two bathrooms. They both had a fireplace in the living room. The old house had a separate dining room, and so did the new house.

   _____

2. The new house looked and felt different from the old house, and Janet did not know if she liked it as much. The old house was nearly one hundred years old. The new house had just been built. Unlike the old two-story house, the new house was all on one level. The hardwood floors at the old house could be seen beneath the old-fashioned rugs, while wall-to-wall carpet covered the floors of the new house.

   _____

# Comparing and Contrasting

A. Imagine that you work for a toy company. You are deciding which of two stuffed rabbits your company should sell. One toy rabbit is tall and thin with long ears that stand up straight. Not fuzzy, this rabbit is wearing a sun hat and appears to be clever and shrewd. The other rabbit is cute and cuddly, with floppy ears. Wearing a fancy, flowered hat, this smiling rabbit is plump. Fill in the chart to describe the rabbits' similarities and differences.

| Category | Rabbit A | Both | Rabbit B |
|---|---|---|---|
| 1. type of animal | | | |
| 2. shape | | | |
| 3. clothes | | | |
| 4. expression | | | |
| 5. ears | | | |

B. Use your chart to answer the questions below.

6.  In what two ways are the stuffed animals alike?

_____

_____

_____

7.  In what two ways are the stuffed animals different?

_____

_____

_____

# Using Enough Details

Read each paragraph. If the paragraph needs more details, choose details from the box below and write them on the lines.

1. The lives of the Pueblo Indians and the Navajo Indians were similar in some ways. They both lived in the Southwest. They both lived in permanent homes.

   _____

   _____

2. Though the Pueblo Indians and the Navajo Indians both lived in the Southwest, their lives were different in some ways. The Pueblo Indians lived in villages called pueblos, with several families in one dwelling. The Navajo Indians lived in scattered hogans.

   _____

   _____

   _____

Pueblos and Navajos also both wove cloth.

The Navajos wove wool, while the Pueblos wove cotton and feathers together.

The Pueblos depended entirely on the crops and the livestock they raised. The Navajos hunted and gathered as well as raised food and livestock.

Both groups of Indians farmed and raised animals.

# Using Effective Transitions

Good writers arrange their ideas carefully and use transition words to show how sentences are related.

Write paragraphs by arranging the sentences of each group in a smooth, logical order. Add any transition words that are needed.

1. Water-skiing is a sport for warm weather.
   The similarity ends there.
   Both water-skiing and snow skiing require skis.
   Snow skiing is a cold-weather sport.
   People snow ski on a mountain slope.
   Water-skiing is done on a large body of water.

   _____

   _____

   _____

   _____

   _____

2. In football, the whole team is in motion on every play.
   When a baseball team is at bat, most of the players
     are sitting and waiting.
   I like playing football better than playing baseball.
   I like to be moving throughout a game.

   _____

   _____

   _____

   _____

   _____

# Proofreading Paragraphs of Comparison and Contrast

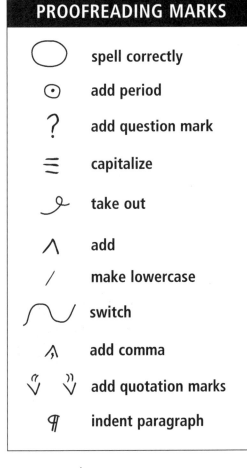

| PROOFREADING MARKS | |
|---|---|
| ◯ | spell correctly |
| ⊙ | add period |
| ? | add question mark |
| ≡ | capitalize |
| ℈ | take out |
| ∧ | add |
| / | make lowercase |
| ∿ | switch |
| ∧ | add comma |
| ⌄ ⌄ | add quotation marks |
| ¶ | indent paragraph |

Proofread the paragraphs of comparison and contrast, paying special attention to subject-verb agreement. Use the Proofreading Marks to correct at least seven errors.

People sometimes asks me who my best friend is. Truthfully, I do not know. I have two close friends, and I like them both very much.

My friends judy and Margie is alike in many ways. Both are intelligent, loyal, and helpful Either can carry on a great conversation. Each has an excellent sense of humor, and they enjoy many of the same activities.

However, my two friends are different in many ways. I has more arguments with Judy. She complains if she does not like something, and she argue if she disagrees with me. Margie rarely complains or argues, so we almost never fights.

On the other hand, Judy is a more honest friend. She always says exactly what she thinks or feels. In contrast, Margie never say anything negative to me about things i have said or done. Instead, she may say something to someone else, and her comments often gets back to me. If Judy has a complaint, she discusses it with the person who has caused the problem.

# Write a Paragraph from Advertisements

Find advertisements for two competing products. Cut out the ads you find. Make a chart that compares the two products. Then, using the information from the chart, write a paragraph of comparison and contrast.

**Four Out of Five Dogs Choose Beddie-By!**

The Softest!
Odorless!
Why pay more?
Pet calming!

| Product 1 | Both | Product 2 |
|---|---|---|
|  |  |  |

_____

_____

_____

_____

_____

_____

# Create a Toy

With a friend, decide on a kind of toy you might design. On separate pieces of paper, each of you draw a picture of your version of the toy. Do not let the other person see it. When both of you are finished, write a paragraph to compare and contrast your drawings. Write at least three similarities and three differences.

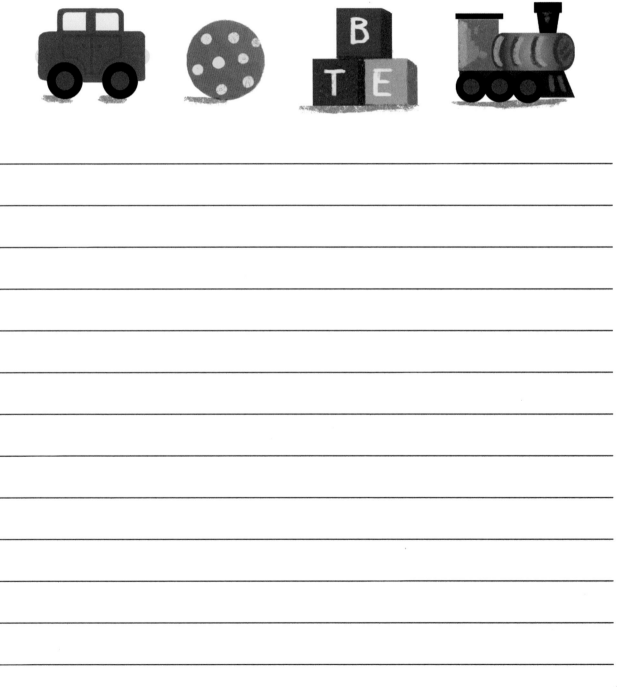

_____

_____

_____

_____

_____

_____

_____

_____

_____

_____

_____

# Compare Sports

Write a paragraph comparing or contrasting two sports. When you revise your paragraph, make sure your transitions are smooth.

# A Practice Compare-and-Contrast Paper

## IN-LINE SKATES AND ICE SKATES

Two fast-moving sports popular with people of all ages are two kinds of skating. They are in-line skating and ice-skating. Whether skaters are on the sidewalk or on the ice, most of them can enjoy hours of fun. That is, of course, if they have the right equipment.

Skaters in both sports use equipment that is alike and different. Both kinds of skates are made for speed. Today's skates let a skater skate well all the time. Skaters can also use their skates in more than one sport. However, certain kinds of skates are made for different uses. They work best when a skater uses the right skate for the right sport. That means, for example, that a hockey player uses skates made for hockey. She can also use them to figure skate. However, in that case, she will probably skate better if she uses skates made for figure skating.

All in-line skates are made for land. So, they all have the same basic features. An in-line skate has a boot that is usually made from plastic. The boot is firm. It holds the skater's ankle comfortably. The boot's lining comes out so it can be washed. On the outside of the boot, there are laces, buckles, or both to fasten the boot.

An ice skate also has a boot, but this boot is made only for ice. The boot is usually made from leather. It provides support for the ankle. It is also designed to be comfortable and warm. The boot's lining is made from a material that helps air move. However, the longer the skater wears these boots, the more likely the skater's feet will perspire. Over time, this can cause the boots to deteriorate, or break down. That makes it important to wipe out the boots after each use.

Both kinds of skates have one or more objects that help the skater move. In-line skates use wheels, usually four. There are three things about the wheels that require the skater's attention. They are size, hardness, and

bearings. To check the size of the wheel, the skater measures the wheel's diameter in millimeters (mm). The size of the wheel is important, because the larger it is, the faster it rolls. Most ordinary in-line skates range from 72 mm to 76 mm. The size is marked on the side of the wheel.

The second important feature of the wheel is its hardness. Wheels are made from a kind of plastic. The hardness of the plastic varies and is measured in durometers. A zero durometer represents the softest plastic. One hundred durometers represent the hardest plastic. The harder the plastic, the faster the skater can go.

The last important feature of a wheel is its bearings. Ball bearings are inside the hubs of the wheels. These ball bearings let the wheels roll. So, the better the ball bearings, the faster the wheels roll.

Instead of wheels, ice skates use blades. Each blade is attached to the sole of the boot with a screw mount. This mount holds the blade tightly in place.

Blades are made of metal, usually stainless steel. Then they are coated with another metal, such as chrome, nickel, or aluminum. The blade is solid and has a toe pick at the front end. The toe pick lets the skater grip the ice. It also helps the skater take off. There is a ridge that runs along the bottom of the blade. This ridge is called the "hollow." The hollow cuts the ice as the skater glides over it.

Being able to stop is important to every skater. Only in-line skates have brakes. A brake pad is attached to the back of each boot. The skater stops by lifting his or her toes and pressing the brake pad to the ground.

For ice skaters, stopping is another matter. There are no brakes on ice skates. Instead, the skater uses his or her legs and feet to stop. The skater presses on the sides of his or her skates to stop.

In-line skating and ice-skating are alike in some ways and different in others. Their differences make both sports interesting to many skaters. The ways they are alike let skaters skate in both sports. For skaters with the right skates, skating is several sports in one.

# Respond to the Practice Paper

Summarize the story by making a chart. Use the chart below to list ways in-line skates and ice skates are alike and different.

### A COMPARE-AND-CONTRAST CHART FOR
### IN-LINE SKATES AND ICE SKATES

| How In-Line Skates and Ice Skates Are Alike | How In-Line Skates and Ice Skates Are Different |
| --- | --- |
|  |  |

# Analyze the Practice Paper

Read "In-line Skates and Ice Skates" again. As you read, think about how the writer achieved his or her purpose for writing. Write your answers to the following questions or directions.

1. When does the writer tell you what this paper is going to be about?

   _____

   _____

   _____

2. Why do you think the writer talks about how in-line skates and ice skates are alike before explaining how they are different?

   _____

   _____

   _____

3. List three differences between in-line skates and ice skates. List them in the order the writer describes them. Explain why you think the writer used this order.

   _____

   _____

   _____

   _____

4. How are the first and last paragraphs related?

   _____

   _____

   _____

   _____

   _____

# Writing Assignment

Think about two sports you would like to write about. Write about how they are alike and how they are different. Use this writing plan to help you write a first draft on page 83.

Choose two sports you want to write about. Call them A and B.

A = _____          B = _____

Use what you know, books, or the Internet to learn more about A and B. Learn about three main ideas: where the sports are played, what equipment players need, and the rules. Under each main idea, list what is true only about A in the A circle. List what is true only about B in the B circle. List what is true about both A and B where the two circles overlap.

**MAIN IDEA:**
Where are the sports played?

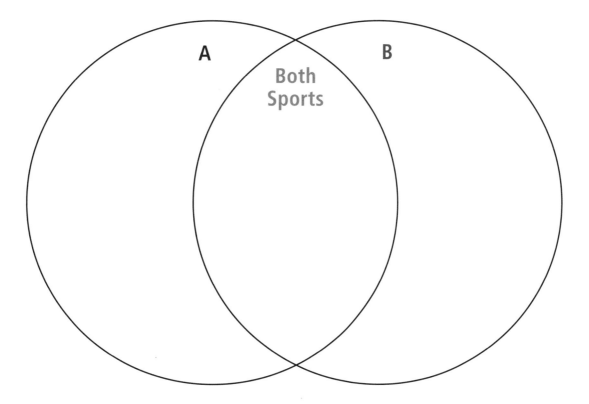

A

Both Sports

B

**MAIN IDEA:**
What equipment do players need?

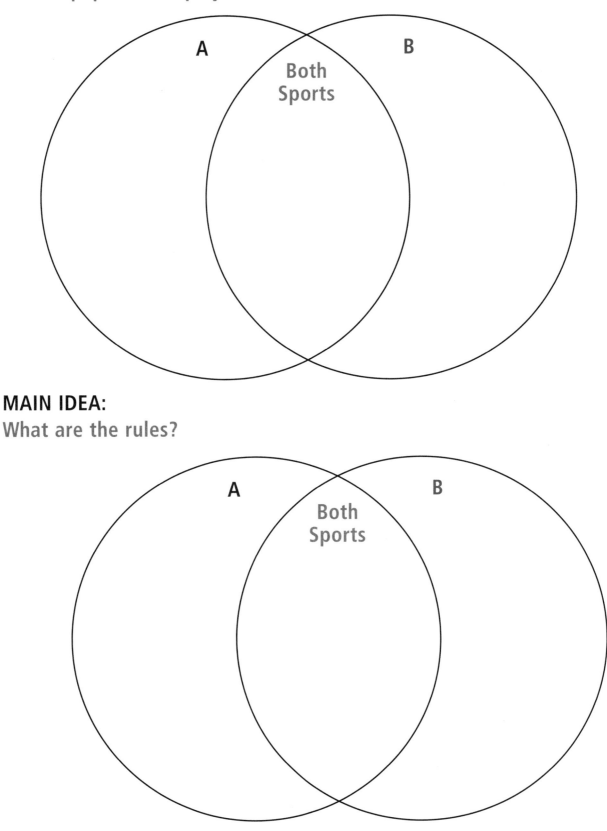

A

B

Both
Sports

**MAIN IDEA:**
What are the rules?

A

B

Both
Sports

# First Draft

TIPS FOR WRITING A COMPARE-AND-CONTRAST PAPER:

- Find information about your sports.
- Organize the information you find into main ideas.
- Use details to explain each main idea.
- Explain how the sports are alike.
- Explain how the sports are different.
- Use your last paragraph to summarize your main ideas in a new way.

Use your writing plan as a guide as you write your first draft of a compare-and-contrast paper. Include a catchy title.

_____

_____

_____

_____

_____

_____

_____

_____

_____

_____

_____

(Continue on your own paper.)

# Revise the Draft

Use the chart below to help you revise your draft. Check YES or NO to answer each question in the chart. If you answer NO, make notes to remind yourself how you can revise, or change, your writing to improve it.

| Question | YES ✔ | NO ✔ | If the answer is NO, what will you do to improve your writing? |
|---|---|---|---|
| Do you introduce the sports you will write about in the first paragraph? | | | |
| Does your paper explain how the two sports are alike? | | | |
| Does your paper explain how the two sports are different? | | | |
| Do you have more than one main idea about each sport? | | | |
| Did you organize the main ideas into paragraphs? | | | |
| Do you use details to support each main idea? | | | |
| Do you summarize the main ideas of your paper in your conclusion? | | | |
| Have you corrected mistakes in spelling, grammar, and punctuation? | | | |

Use the notes in your chart and your writing plan to revise your draft.

# Writing Report Card

Read your revised draft again or ask someone else to read it. Have the person who reads your paper complete the following Report Card. Revise your paper until you have no less than a Very Good Score for each item.

Title of paper: _____

Purpose of paper: _____*This paper compares and contrasts two sports.*_____

Person who scores the paper: _____

| Score | Writing Goals |
|-------|---------------|
| | Does the writer tell what the paper will be about in the first paragraph? |
| | Does the paper explain how two sports are alike? |
| | Does the paper explain how the two sports are different? |
| | Does the writer use more than one main idea to show the important ways the sports are alike and different? |
| | Does the writer organize the paragraphs in a way that makes sense? |
| | Does the writer use important details to support each main idea? |
| | Does the last paragraph summarize what the paper is about? |
| | Are the paper's grammar, spelling, and punctuation correct? |

☺ Excellent Score    ☆ Very Good Score    + Good Score
✔ Acceptable Score    − Needs Improvement

# UNIT 5: Persuasive Writing

## HOW MUCH DO YOU KNOW?

**A. Read the following statements from a persuasive essay. Write the word or the group of words from the box that best describes the techniques used in the statement.**

testimonial                     emotional words

faulty generalization           bandwagon technique

1. Instead of mindless wasting of energy, energy-hogs must use less energy.

   _____

2. An expert from Nevada explained that when rivers are dammed for water power, it destroys beautiful valleys.

   _____

3. Nuclear power plants help solve energy problems, but the storage of huge amounts of radioactive wastes only makes the problem so much worse than anyone can imagine.

   _____

4. Fuels made from fossils pollute the air, so people should recycle more.

   _____

**B. Read the following statements. After each sentence, write _fact_ or _opinion_.**

5. Even the manufacturing of equipment for other sources of energy uses energy and creates pollution in the process.

   _____

6. The best way to use less energy is to walk or ride a bike.

   _____

# Analyzing a Persuasive Essay

> **A PERSUASIVE ESSAY**
> - gives an opinion about an issue
> - gives facts and reasons to back up the opinion
> - has an introductory paragraph, supporting paragraphs, and a conclusion

Read the following statements from a persuasive essay. Write the word or the group of words from the box on page 86 that best describes the techniques used in the statement.

1. We have to keep greedy builders from gobbling up our wilderness to make a buck.

   _____

2. Jack Tenor, the famous athlete, says that they passed a similar law in his town and everyone is happy with it.

   _____

3. Join the thousands of people all over the country who are demanding laws to restrict building in their area.

   _____

4. Since my neighbors like my idea, we're sure that this is what the community wants.

   _____

5. Do not trade the unspoiled beauty and the restful peace of the country for the crowded, smoggy rat race of the city.

   _____

6. Maria Gomez, a university professor, says that life in the city can be difficult.

   _____

# Classifying Fact and Opinion

**TO WRITE A PERSUASIVE ESSAY, GOOD WRITERS**

- back up opinions with facts

- keep opinions and facts separated

Read the following dialogue. Before each sentence, write *fact* if the speaker has expressed a fact. Write *opinion* if the speaker has expressed an opinion. If the speaker has used a signal word, underline that word in the sentence.

1. _____ "Quite a few people say they have seen the Loch Ness monster," said Rita.

2. _____ "That many people can't be wrong," said Richard.

3. _____ "Aw, they're all a bunch of cranks," said Craig.

4. _____ "Yes," said Bob. "They should be ignored."

5. _____ "It's people like you who ought to be ignored," responded Joe.

6. _____ "Nobody has proved that there is a monster," Bill pointed out.

7. _____ "Yes," agreed Nancy. "A hundred and fifty years ago, scientists didn't believe the giant squid existed."

8. _____ "Probably most people wouldn't believe in elephants if scientists hadn't seen them," commented Jill.

9. _____ "That's silly!" said Tracy. "I'm sure they would."

10. _____ "Loch Ness is deeper than other lakes in the area," said Ray.

11. _____ "It has not been completely explored," added David.

# Using Vivid Words

> Good writers use vivid words and phrases.

Rewrite the following statements from a persuasive essay about the evils of slavery. Replace each word or phrase in parentheses ( ) with one from the box.

| | | |
|---|---|---|
| chained to their masters | demand | lashed |
| crush out | auctioned | disgraceful |
| track down | labor | mock |

1. How can a planet such as Theron still tolerate the (wrong) laws that permit slavery in the year 3045?

   _____

2. The Theronites should (request) an end to that practice.

   _____

3. Thousands of Robots are (made slaves) by existing laws.

   _____

4. The Robots (work) from dawn until midnight without pay.

   _____

5. Robot catchers are hired to (find) escaping Robots.

   _____

6. To be a truly modern planet, Theron should (end) practices that deny freedom to all Theronites.

   _____

# Varying Sentence Structure and Length

> Good writers make their compositions more interesting by varying the length and the structure of their sentences.

Rewrite each paragraph. Create sentence variety by combining sentences, adding words, and shifting the placement of words.

1. I think people should use less energy. It is important that they do this. Every kind of energy costs us something. Fuels made from fossils are in short supply. They also pollute the air.

   _____

   _____

   _____

2. Other sources of energy also have drawbacks. Water power requires damming rivers. This has destroyed many beautiful valleys. Even manufacturing the equipment for other sources of power uses energy. It creates pollution, too. We should cut our use of energy. We can avoid many harmful results of our present overuse of it.

   _____

   _____

   _____

   _____

   _____

# Proofreading a Persuasive Essay

Proofread this beginning of a persuasive essay, paying special attention to the capitalization of proper nouns. Use the Proofreading Marks to correct at least eight errors.

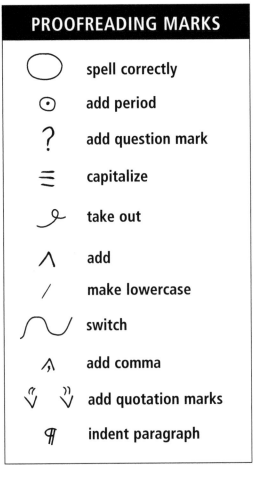

**PROOFREADING MARKS**

| | |
|---|---|
| ◯ | spell correctly |
| ⊙ | add period |
| ? | add question mark |
| = | capitalize |
| ℘ | take out |
| ∧ | add |
| / | make lowercase |
| ∿ | switch |
| ∧ | add comma |
| ⌄ ⌄ | add quotation marks |
| ¶ | indent paragraph |

The people of the World are faced with alarming environmental problems. I am convinced that we must all cooperate through international agencys to solve these problems. Working alone, one state or one nation cannot protect its land and people from environmental hazards. The problems faced by people in the united states are also problems for people in canada, Japan, and russia. Only by facing these problems together and trying to work out cooperative

solutions can we protect ourselves and our Planet.

There are several reasons why international cooperation is needed. in the first place, some environmental dangers threaten the whole plant rather than local areas. Damage to the ozone layer is a good example. If someone in nebraska uses an aerosol spray, the chemicals do not stay in Nebraska. Those damaging chemicals travel to the ozone layer, where they affect the whole world. Therefore, a State or Country cannot protect itself against ozone damage simply by passing a law forbidding the local use of aerosols.

# List Steps to Save Energy

With a friend or two, list 10 specific steps to save energy. Use the ideas in your list to write a persuasive essay about energy conservation.

_____    _____

_____    _____

_____    _____

_____    _____

_____    _____

_____

_____

_____

_____

_____

_____

# Vote for a Persuasive Essay Topic

Vote on each issue below. Then pick one issue that you feel strongly about. Write a persuasive essay on that issue. Read your essay to a friend.

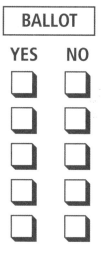

| BALLOT | | |
|---|---|---|
| YES | NO | Check one box. |
| ☐ | ☐ | All city parks should have an area for exercising dogs. |
| ☐ | ☐ | The school basketball courts should be open at night. |
| ☐ | ☐ | The school cafeteria should serve vegetarian lunches. |
| ☐ | ☐ | All students should wear uniforms to school. |
| ☐ | ☐ | Girls and boys should be allowed to play on the same school basketball teams. |

_____

_____

_____

_____

_____

_____

_____

_____

_____

_____

_____

# Writing from a Picture

Look at each of the pictures below. Write a statement of opinion about each picture. Choose one of the opinions and write a persuasive essay to persuade your friends to accept your opinion.

_____

_____

_____

_____

_____

_____

_____

_____

_____

_____

_____

_____

_____

_____

_____

_____

_____

_____

_____

# Take Opposing Views

Think about some issues about which you haven't made up your mind, and then write down both sides of the issue. With a friend, find facts and reasons to support each side. Choose one side and write a persuasive essay on it. Read your essay to your friend. Here are examples of possible issues:

"All children should be in bed by 9:30 on school nights."

"Childen should be allowed to go to bed whenever they want."

ISSUE: _____

_____

SIDE 1:                       SIDE 2:

_____   _____

_____   _____

_____   _____

_____

_____

_____

_____

_____

_____

_____

_____

# A Practice Persuasive Movie Review

## BERNIE, THE LAUGHING OGRE

If a story needs one hero, one princess in distress, and one villain, or evil force, to be a fairy tale, then *Bernie, the Laughing Ogre* may be one of the funniest fairy tales you've ever seen. That's right, the word is *seen*, not *heard*. Because *Bernie, the Laughing Ogre* is a movie, and its characters are unlike any fairy tale characters you've ever met before.

Let's start with the hero, Bernie. Bernie is tall, but definitely not handsome. In fact, he's a chubby, purple giant with too much hair. Most of the time, too much hair on a giant isn't a problem. But Bernie's hair grows in all the wrong places. There's hair between his toes and fingers. There's even hair growing from his nose and ears, but there's no hair on his head. Bernie is bald.

There's something else that makes Bernie an uncommon hero. He's ticklish. A single scratch on his purple skin makes Bernie lose control. He falls to the ground, laughing and gasping for air. Bernie knows this is unacceptable behavior for a giant. In fact, his giant friends have threatened to kick Bernie out of their drama club if he can't be more serious. Bernie wants to act like other giants, but he can't help himself.

To be safe, Bernie never goes into the nearby village where he might rub up against the moles. That may not seem so funny, but you need to remember that moles are hairy and blind. They use their whiskers to see. Their short, stubby whiskers are always moving about. If you're a bald, ticklish giant like Bernie, you can see why moles might be a problem. In fact, Bernie avoids moles altogether. That includes princess moles.

The princess in this story is no ordinary fairy-tale princess. For one thing, she's a mole. For the second thing, she's not really in distress. She's used to the dull, dark castle where she lives. She's also used to the boring dragon that holds her captive. Princess Stella has learned to make herself laugh, but only when the dragon isn't around. Nothing makes the dragon angrier than laughter. The first time the princess laughed, the dragon shook and shivered. Steam came from its ears. Its skin turned from blue to red. This made the princess laugh, too. That made the dragon even more furious. The princess soon realized that of all the dragons in the world, she got the one without a sense of humor. That's when she decided to find a way out of the castle. Plus, she worried about the moles in her village. What was the villain Manco doing to them?

Manco is like most of the villains you read about in fairy tales. He never smiles unless he's being wicked. Nothing makes him happier than making someone else unhappy. That's why he let the dragon into the village to kidnap the princess. He knew that once the princess was gone, everyone in the village would be sad. That's where Bernie's problem begins.

Most of the time, no one comes near the dark, unfriendly forest where Bernie lives. Until the moles come, that is. You see, some of the moles decide they need a giant to help them rescue their princess and bring laughter back to the village. Their first stop is Bernie's forest.

Unless Bernie agrees to help, the moles tell him more moles will come. Bernie has no choice. He must say yes or risk becoming the laughingstock of giants everywhere. So, Bernie agrees to rescue the princess if the moles promise to return home. The moles promise, but that's not exactly what happens.

I could tell you more, but I don't want to spoil the surprises that fill this movie. Don't think about how Bernie helps all of those hairy, whiskered moles rescue the princess. Don't imagine what the dragon does the first time it hears Bernie laugh. You'll see how Bernie handles these problems when you see the movie. Right now, I'd like to talk about something else that's going to make you love this fairy tale.

*Bernie, the Laughing Ogre*, the movie, is an example of the best of computer technology. The people who brought these characters to life have done something extraordinary. Each character walks, talks, and looks like a real living thing. When Bernie smiles, you see wrinkles in his skin. When the wind blows, you see each mole whisker twitch. When the dragon breathes fire, you almost feel the flames. Characters look so real, you're sure they are.

There are hundreds of reasons why you should see *Bernie, the Laughing Ogre*. There's not a single reason not to see it. This story isn't like the fairy tales you read when you were a child. It will make you laugh. You'll also be amazed by the computer magic that made this movie. See the movie now. Then you can make plans to see it a second time because I'm sure you will.

# Respond to the Practice Paper

Write your answers to the following questions or directions.

1. Why is the hero uncommon?

   _____

   _____

2. Besides the hero, who are the other important characters in this movie?

   _____

   _____

3. Describe the plot of the movie in one or two sentences.

   _____

   _____

   _____

4. Write a paragraph to summarize *Bernie, the Laughing Ogre*. Use these questions to help you write your summary:

   • What is the purpose of this paper?
   • What reasons does the writer give for seeing this movie?

   _____

   _____

   _____

   _____

   _____

   _____

   _____

# Analyze the Practice Paper

Read *Bernie, the Laughing Ogre* again. As you read, think about the reasons the writer gives to convince readers to see this movie. Write your answers to the following questions.

1. How does the writer use the first paragraph to grab the reader's attention?

_____

_____

_____

_____

2. Read paragraph 9 again. Why do you think the writer included this paragraph?

_____

_____

_____

_____

3. The writer uses most of the review to talk about the characters and plot. Why do you think the writer includes paragraph 10?

_____

_____

_____

_____

4. What do the first and last paragraphs have in common?

_____

_____

_____

_____

# Writing Assignment

In a persuasive movie review, writers try to convince readers to watch a movie. What's your favorite movie? Write a persuasive movie review to convince your friends to see this movie. Use this writing plan to help you write a first draft on the next page.

**What is the name of the movie you will review?**

Write reasons your friends should see this movie.
Write details to support each reason.

**Reason #1**

Details to support Reason #1

**Reason #2**

Details to support Reason #2

**Reason #3**

Details to support Reason #3

**Reason #4**

Details to support Reason #4

# First Draft

TIPS FOR WRITING A PERSUASIVE MOVIE REVIEW:

- Make sure you have a strong opinion.
- Give good reasons to support your opinion.
- Give important details that support each reason.
- Grab your reader's attention in the first paragraph.
- Restate your opinion in the last paragraph.

Use your writing plan as a guide for writing your first draft of a persuasive movie review. Include a catchy title.

_____

_____

_____

_____

_____

_____

_____

_____

_____

_____

_____

(Continue on your own paper.)

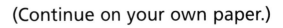

# Revise the Draft

Use the chart below to help you revise your draft. Check YES or NO to answer each question in the chart. If you answer NO, make notes to remind yourself how you can revise, or change, your writing to improve it.

| Question | YES ✔ | NO ✔ | If the answer is NO, what will you do to improve your writing? |
|---|---|---|---|
| Do you use your first paragraph to grab the reader's attention? | | | |
| Do you make it clear that you have a strong opinion? | | | |
| Do you give good reasons to support your opinion? | | | |
| Do you include details that help support each reason? | | | |
| Do you restate your opinion in the last paragraph? | | | |
| Does this review make your reader want to see the movie? | | | |
| Have you corrected mistakes in spelling, grammar, and punctuation? | | | |

Use the notes in your chart and your writing plan to revise your draft.

# Writing Report Card

Read your revised draft again or ask someone else to read it. Have the person who reads your paper complete the following Report Card. Revise your paper until you have no less than a Very Good Score for each item.

Title of paper: _____

Purpose of paper: _*This paper is a persuasive movie review.*_____

Person who scores the paper: _____

| Score | Writing Goals |
|---|---|
|  | Does the first paragraph grab the reader's attention? |
|  | Is the writer's opinion clearly stated? |
|  | Does the writer give good reasons for his or her opinion? |
|  | Are there details to support each reason? |
|  | Does the writer restate his or her opinion in the last paragraph? |
|  | Does this review make you want to see the movie? |
|  | Are the review's grammar, spelling, and punctuation correct? |

☺ Excellent Score    ☆ Very Good Score    + Good Score
✔ Acceptable Score    − Needs Improvement

# UNIT 6: Short Report

## HOW MUCH DO YOU KNOW?

Read the following sentences. Mark where each would best fit in a research report about Marco Polo.

1. This is why Marco Polo became famous.
   - ____ a. introduction
   - ____ b. body
   - ____ c. conclusion

2. Shortly thereafter, Marco was captured and imprisoned for a short time.
   - ____ a. introduction
   - ____ b. body
   - ____ c. conclusion

3. Marco returned from China 25 years later.
   - ____ a. introduction
   - ____ b. body
   - ____ c. conclusion

4. For almost 300 years, *The Travels of Marco Polo* stood alone as the only Western description of Asia!
   - ____ a. introduction
   - ____ b. body
   - ____ c. conclusion

5. Marco Polo made his first trip to China when he was 17 years old – a trip that changed his life.
   - ____ a. introduction
   - ____ b. body
   - ____ c. conclusion

# Analyzing a Short Report

A SHORT REPORT
- gives information about a topic
- draws facts from various sources
- has an introduction, a body, and a conclusion

Read the following sentences. Label each one *introduction, body*, or *conclusion* to identify where it would best fit in a short report about peanuts. Tell why you labeled each as you did.

1. George Washington Carver studied the peanut.

   _____

2. Many regions in the southern United States grow peanuts.

   _____

3. Did you know that peanuts are used in making dynamite?

   _____

4. Some farmers grow peanuts to put nitrogen into the soil.

   _____

5. Did you know that the peanut is not a nut?

   _____

6. A pound of peanuts has as much protein as a pound of beef.

   _____

7. As you can see, the peanut is a valuable product with many uses.

   _____

8. Some inks contain peanut products.

   _____

9. Peanut meal makes excellent feed for livestock.

   _____

10. Knowing all these uses, aren't you glad that people learned to cultivate peanuts?

    _____

# Connecting Ideas in a Summary

> **TO WRITE A SUMMARY, GOOD WRITERS**
> - state the most important points about a subject
> - retell a story or an article briefly
> - use their own words without changing the meaning

**A. Read the following report. Then read the numbered statements that follow. Underline each statement that should be included in a summary of the report.**

It was 6:30 P.M. in Cottonville. The townspeople were going quietly about their business. The Johnsons were just sitting down to dinner. The Garcias were watching the news. Commuters all over the city were still on their way home from work. At 6:31, the earthquake hit. It measured 5.5 on the Richter scale. Some people rushed to stand in doorways or crawl under tables. After the earth had stopped shaking, people waited nervously to see if there would be more shocks. No deaths were reported, but a few people suffered minor injuries.

1. An earthquake occurred in Cottonville.
2. It happened at 6:31 P.M.
3. The Johnsons were sitting down to dinner.
4. The earthquake measured 5.5 on the Richter scale.
5. Some people stood in doorways.
6. There were no deaths.

**B. Write a summary for the original source material below.**

| ORIGINAL SOURCE | SUMMARY |
|---|---|
| Young children learn through play. They may use blocks, toy vehicles, or costumes. Wise parents and teachers provide many opportunities for a variety of play experiences. These will include solitary play as well as play with friends. | _____<br>_____<br>_____<br>_____<br>_____<br>_____<br>_____ |

# Catching the Reader's Interest

GOOD WRITERS

- begin with a striking sentence
- use concrete details
- use quotations

Read the following sentences from a short report. On the lines below, write the striking sentence that would make a good beginning. Then write the numbers of the concrete details and the quotation.

1. In the United States insects are sometimes sold in cans. Bees and ants may be roasted in oil. Caterpillars and other insects may be covered with chocolate.
2. Birds eat insects, too.
3. People eat all kinds of different foods.
4. My grandfather used to threaten to make grasshopper gravy, just as other people do around the world.
5. He was right. In some cultures people do eat locusts.
6. Termite grubs are eaten in many countries. They taste like pork skins when fried.
7. Although insects are a common food in some parts of the world, canned insects are rare and expensive in the United States and not very popular.
8. In areas where insects are a major food source, people do not cover them in chocolate.
9. Dr. Reiner, the famous anthropologist, says, "It makes sense to eat insects because they are far more plentiful than other animals."
10. Of course, these people eat other things, too.

Striking beginning: _____

_____

Concrete details: _____

Quotation: _____

# Combining to Embed a Word or Phrase

> Good writers sometimes embed a word or a phrase from one sentence in another sentence.

Combine the sentences in each pair by embedding a word or a phrase. The first one is done for you.

1. In the eighteenth and nineteenth centuries, the way people did their work changed. It changed dramatically.

   *In the eighteenth and nineteenth centuries, the way people did*

   *their work changed dramatically.*

2. During this period a new society was created. The period was the Industrial Revolution.

   _____

3. A spinner invented a new spinning machine. His name was James Hargreaves.

   _____

4. The new machine could spin eight threads at once. It was called the spinning jenny.

   _____

5. Edmund Cartwright invented a loom. It was operated by water power.

   _____

6. Eli Whitney invented a cotton gin. He invented it in 1793.

   _____

# Proofreading a Short Report

**PROOFREADING HINT**

To be a good proofreader, look for one type of error at a time. For example, proofread once for capitalization errors, once for punctuation errors, and once for spelling errors.

Proofread the beginning of the short report, paying special attention to sentence fragments and run-on sentences. Use the Proofreading Marks to correct at least seven errors.

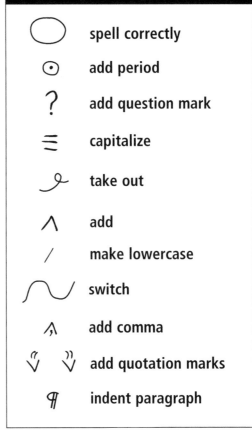

**PROOFREADING MARKS**

- ⬭    spell correctly
- ⊙    add period
- ?    add question mark
- ≡    capitalize
- ℘    take out
- ∧    add
- /    make lowercase
- ∿    switch
- ∧    add comma
- ⌄ ⌄    add quotation marks
- ¶    indent paragraph

Can you imagine an animal that seems to be part mammal? Part reptile, and part bird? If you succeed, you will probably imagine an animal very much like the duckbill, also called a platypus.

Animals that bear their young alive and nurse their young are classified. As mammals. Duckbills nurse their young as mammals do, but they lay eggs as birds do. Although scientists

classify the duckbill as a kind of mammmil, it has characteristics of other animal groups.

In appearance, the duckbill most closely resembles a duck like a duck, it has a large bill it also has webbed feet, fur, and a flat tail like a beaver's.

Most mammals are warm-blooded. Their body temperature remains the same regardless of the temperature. Of their surroundings. A duckbill is cold-blooded like a reptile its body temperature changes with the temperature of its surroundings.

Duckbills die. In captivity, so they must be studied in their natural homes.

# Write about Life in the 1700s

Imagine that you are a reporter in the 1700s. Write a research report about a day in the life of a weaver, a farmer, or a blacksmith. Make sure you have an introduction, a body, and a conclusion.

_____

_____

_____

_____

_____

_____

_____

_____

_____

_____

_____

_____

_____

_____

_____

_____

_____

_____

# Write about History

Imagine that you are Florence Nightingale. You have arrived at a hospital for wounded soldiers. Research Florence Nightingale and nursing practices during the Crimean War. Write a report of conditions you found in the hospital.

_____

_____

_____

_____

_____

_____

_____

_____

_____

_____

_____

_____

_____

_____

_____

_____

# Use a Picture for Writing Ideas

Look at the pictures below. List all the ideas you can think of in connection with each of these pictures. For example, a picture of a horse might make you think of farming, horse racing, and the constellation Pegasus. Then pick one topic and write a short report on it.

_____     _____

_____     _____

_____     _____

_____

_____

_____

_____

_____

_____

_____

_____

_____

# A Practice Short Report

## WHY DO BATS SING?

One day in December 1994, Barbara French began her daily routine. You might be surprised to learn what kind of routine she keeps. She takes care of bats. Barbara's bats are Mexican free-tailed bats (*Tadarida brasiliensis*). The bats she cares for have been hurt and cannot return to the wild. Barbara thought this December day would be like any other, but it wasn't. She got a real surprise. The surprise was the beginning of a scientific discovery.

As Barbara fed the bats, she heard an unfamiliar, bird-like song. She stopped to listen. She heard all of the normal sounds. She recognized Hannah's buzz. Hannah buzzes when she defends her favorite roosting spot. Then Barbara heard Wheatley's squeal. She could tell that another bat had chased him away from the mealworm tray. Barbara also heard the chirp Amy makes when she wants to be fed by hand. But she had never heard this new song before.

Barbara decided to solve the mystery. Whenever she heard the song, Barbara popped her head into the bat cage. As soon as her head was inside the cage, the singing stopped. It took Barbara two weeks to find the singing bat. The singer was Hank, an adult male. He seemed to be singing to a small group of females in his roosting pocket. A roosting pocket is a handmade fabric pouch, or bag, in the bats' cage.

In the following weeks, the male bats became unusually bold and ready to fight. They chased each other all the time. Free-tailed bats usually like the company of other bats, so Barbara thought this behavior was odd. Ordinarily, the bats like to roost together.

Barbara was worried by this change in the bats' behavior. Her familiar little bat colony was suddenly very different. The bats had been happy with each other for the past year. Of course, they sometimes squabbled, pushed, shoved, and swatted at each other. However, these were normal bat behaviors. Plus, the bats always settled their differences quickly. They didn't hurt each other. The bat that started a fight usually tried to end the fight. He or she would snuggle up with the other bats. It was as if the bat wanted to say it was sorry. The entire colony seemed to work together to keep the peace. However, Hank was different.

One day Barbara watched Hank attack Joshua, another bat. Hank darted from his pocket. He buzzed loudly and chased Joshua around the cage. Barbara decided Joshua had probably moved too near Hank's territory. Before Barbara could stop him, Hank caught Joshua and snagged his ear. Hank's anger bothered Barbara, but what followed really upset her. Moments after she had rescued Joshua, he squeezed out of her hand. Joshua zoomed back into Hank's territory. Joshua seemed ready to fight back.

Because she didn't understand the bats' new behaviors, Barbara decided to ask for help. She called Amanda Lollar. Amanda is a licensed expert in the care of captive Mexican free-tailed bats. Amanda told Barbara that Hank was probably "singing to his women." Amanda also told Barbara to watch for pups that would probably be born during the summer. Barbara was surprised that the explanation was so simple. The bats that Barbara cared for would never be wild again. Their problems made it impossible for them to care for themselves. Barbara didn't think that the bats were strong enough to have healthy pups.

The problems were not over. Barbara and the other bats found Hank's behavior too hard to manage. Hank fought with other males all the time. He bit Joshua's ear again. He even tried to attack Barbara as she fed a female.

Barbara noticed something new. Three females that had been

roosting with Hank suddenly began eating more. They ate everything Barbara fed them and wanted more.

Finally, Hank's singing stopped. The females left Hank and moved into Wheatley's roosting area. Eventually, Hank became himself again. The Hank problem was solved, but a Wheatley problem began. Wheatley began to guard the females that were expecting babies. Wheatley became as fierce as Hank had been.

In June, as Barbara was feeding the bats, she saw a little pink pup about the size of a walnut. Although the baby was very young, it was able to follow its mother around inside the roosting pocket. Twelve days later, Barbara saw the birth of a second pup. This baby was born with its eyes open. It was able to lick its tiny wings clean within minutes after birth.

Barbara learned a lot from her experience with her bats. So did scientists who study bats. Barbara was able to give scientists information they had never had before. Hank's music wasn't a mystery anymore. Neither was Wheatley's protective behavior. Thanks to Barbara and her bats, scientists now know much more about the mating behaviors of Mexican free-tailed bats.

# Respond to the Practice Paper

Write your answers to the following questions or directions.

1. Why was Barbara surprised the first time she heard a bat sing?

   _____

   _____

2. Why was Barbara surprised when the male bats became more willing to fight?

   _____

   _____

3. Why did Barbara contact Amanda Lollar?

   _____

   _____

4. Write a paragraph to summarize the report. Use these questions to help you write your summary:

   • What are the main ideas in this report?
   • How did Amanda explain Hank's behavior?
   • What did scientists learn from Barbara's experience?

   _____

   _____

   _____

   _____

   _____

   _____

   _____

   _____

# Analyze the Practice Paper

Read "Why Do Bats Sing?" again. As you read, think about the main ideas the writer tells about. Write your answers to the following questions.

1. Which paragraph did the writer use to tell you what this report was going to be about?

   _____

   _____

2. Read the second paragraph again. What details did the writer use to explain why the singing was unusual?

   _____

   _____

3. Read the fifth and sixth paragraphs again. How does the sixth paragraph support the fifth paragraph?

   _____

   _____

   _____

   _____

   _____

4. How is the first paragraph related to the last paragraph?

   _____

   _____

   _____

   _____

   _____

# Writing Assignment

In a short report, writers write about one topic. They find information about the topic. Then they use the information to choose the main ideas for their report. They also choose details to help explain each main idea. Write a short report about a science topic that interests you. Your idea might even come from the report "Why Do Bats Sing?" Use this writing plan to help you write a first draft on the next page.

The topic of this paper is:

_____

Main Idea of Paragraph 1: _____

Detail: _____

Detail: _____

Detail: _____


Main Idea of Paragraph 2: _____

Detail: _____

Detail: _____

Detail: _____


Main Idea of Paragraph 3: _____

Detail: _____

Detail: _____

Detail: _____

# First Draft

TIPS FOR WRITING A SHORT REPORT:

- Find information about your topic.
- Take notes about main ideas important to your topic.
- Take notes about important details for each main idea.
- Organize the main ideas and the details into paragraphs.
- Put paragraphs in a logical order.
- Use the last paragraph to summarize your report.

Use your writing plan as a guide as you write your first draft of a short report. Include a catchy title.

_____

(Continue on your own paper.)

# Revise the Draft

Use the chart below to help you revise your draft. Check YES or NO to answer each question in the chart. If you answer NO, make notes to remind yourself how you can revise, or change, your writing to improve it.

| Question | YES ✔ | NO ✔ | If the answer is NO, what will you do to improve your writing? |
|---|---|---|---|
| Does your report focus on one topic? | | | |
| Do you introduce your topic in the first paragraph? | | | |
| Do you have more than one main idea to explain your topic? | | | |
| Do you organize your main ideas into paragraphs? | | | |
| Do you include details to explain each main idea? | | | |
| Do you use your last paragraph to summarize your report? | | | |
| Have you corrected mistakes in spelling, grammar, and punctuation? | | | |

Use the notes in your chart and your writing plan to revise your draft.

# Writing Report Card

Read your revised draft again or ask someone else to read it. Have the person who reads your paper complete the following Report Card. Revise your paper until you have no less than a Very Good Score for each item.

Title of paper: _____

Purpose of paper: _*This paper is a short report.*_____

Person who scores the paper: _____

| Score | Writing Goals |
|---|---|
| | Does this short report focus on one topic? |
| | Does the writer introduce the topic of this paper in the first paragraph? |
| | Does the writer use more than one main idea to explain the topic? |
| | Are main ideas organized into paragraphs? |
| | Are there details to explain each main idea? |
| | Does the report "stick" to the topic? |
| | Does the last paragraph summarize the report? |
| | Are the report's grammar, spelling, and punctuation correct? |

☺ Excellent Score     ☆ Very Good Score     + Good Score
✔ Acceptable Score     − Needs Improvement

# Answer Key

Answers to the practice paper exercises questions may vary, but examples are provided here to give you an idea of how your child may respond.

**Unit 1: Personal Narrative**

**p. 6**
1. first person 2. A fire broke out in Uncle Mike's apartment building. Answers will vary but should show cause/effect from story.

**p. 7**
1. first person; my, I, me 2. excited, but not expecting to be surprised 3. The writer became surprised. 4. a. The family gathered after dinner.–first b. The writer opened the first gift. c. The writer heard a rustling noise.–after d. The writer noticed that a box moved.–a minute later e. Father picked up the present.–then

**p. 8–9**
people headed for the beach, which caused traffic to be jammed, which caused overheated cars, which caused people to become hot and thirsty, which caused people to stop at juice bar, which caused increased business

**p. 10**
1. right number 2. too many–Possible responses to cross out: My mother refused to buy me a horse. I had to iron my shirt. Joan won the spelling bee, and I only came in second. 3. too few–Accept one or two examples of Wayne's ideas.

**p. 11**
Possible responses: 1. The Ross family left their apartment house early. 2. The children climbed into the car enthusiastically. 3. Bill Ross was the motorist for the first thirty minutes. 4. He had just finished a course in driving at school. 5. Bill and his father switched places before they reached the mountains. 6. The scent of pines was everywhere. 7. Bill and Susan immediately went for a hike.

**p. 12–13**
What an amazing experience my brothers and I had with the wind last (autunm!) [autumn] We had driven with our parents to Point Reyes, north of San francisco. Point Reyes is known as one of the (windyest) [windiest] spots in the (cuontry,) [country] and on that day the winds were raging up to 50 miles an hour all along the California coast.

I had no way of determining the speed of the wind at Point reyes that afternoon. I can only tell you that when we jumped into the air, we were blown a full five feet before landing⊙ The wind picked us up and carried us with the force of (rushhing) [rushing] water. we [we] (simply) [simply] could not fall backward. The wind was so strong that we could lean back against it and let it support us as firmly as a brick wall would.

My brothers and I decided to take a short walk downwind along the beach. We allowed the wind to push us along at a (rappid) [rapid] pace. For a while we (stoped) [stopped] walking altogether. We simply jumped into the air, let ourselves be blown along like empty milk (cartoons,) [cartons] and landed. Then we jumped into the air again. Borne by the wind, we progressed as quickly as if we had been walking⊙

**p. 21**
1. The writer learned how to swim. 2. The main setting for this story is the Llano River. The cool river has fast rapids, shallow places, and deep swimming holes that feel good when the hot sun is beating down. 3. In the second paragraph, the writer tells us that J.W. is loud, funny, and a real pain. 4. The writer is surprised when Donnie offers to teach him to swim, so they probably don't do a lot of things together. You can tell he cares about him, though, because he talks to him when he is sitting by herself and he is patient with him as he practices each step. I think the writer trusts Donnie and looks up to him. 5. Check to see that your child summarizes the significant events of the story. Summaries should be organized in a thoughtful way, with the main ideas and important details clearly presented.

**p. 22**
1. The writer uses dialogue and vivid descriptions to show emotion. 2. Reading exactly what J.W. says instead of a description helps us understand why the writer was so embarrassed. 3. The writer adds funny comments to help readers picture what is going on and to help us understand her personality. Humor keeps the reader interested in the story. 4. For the most part, the writer uses dialogue to help the reader picture J.W. She gives examples of how he teased him and how he complimented him on learning to swim.

**Unit 2: How-to Writing**

**p. 27**
It's often not easy to give a dog a pill, but with the help of a little tuna fish, it can be done. You will need the pill, a can of tuna, and a plate. First, make a small ball of tuna around the pill. Next, put the tuna ball on a plate. Sit at the kitchen table and pretend to eat the tuna ball. Finally, casually drop the ball of tuna on the floor. The dog will eat the tuna and never realize the pill was inside! Materials: the pill, a can of tuna, a plate

**p. 28**
If you ever need to warm your body when you are chilled, you should try making some ginger tea. You will need a fresh ginger root, three cups of water, a knife, and a glass pot or kettle. First, put three cups of water into the glass pot. Next, cut six slices of ginger root. The slices should be $\frac{1}{8}$ to $\frac{1}{4}$ inch thick. Add the ginger to the water in the pot. Boil the ginger, letting the water evaporate until only one cup of water remains. Strain the ginger tea into a cup. Drink it hot.

**p. 29–30**
Materials: orange juice, bowl, green drink mix, spoon, pineapple sherbet, lemon soda. Steps: 1. Pour orange juice into bowl. 2. Add green drink mix. 3. Add sherbet in small scoops. 4. Stir until some sherbet melts. 5. Add lemon soda.

**p. 31**
a. for a sixth-grader b. for a second-grader The second paragraph used shorter sentences and explained how the trick works.

**p. 32**
Possible responses: 1. If you are thirsty, you can make a refreshing yogurt shake. 2. First, measure two tablespoons of plain yogurt into a blender. 3. Next, add two tablespoons of fruit juice. 4. Add one-half teaspoon of honey. 5. Add one-third of a banana. 6. Add a pinch of nutmeg to the other ingredients. 7. Crush two ice cubes and add them to the mixture. 8. Blend the ingredients until they are frothy.

**p. 33–34**
With the help of a little tuna fish and some acting skill, you can easily get your dog Titan to take his pill. As you know, Titan often begs for tuna, but you never give him

any. If you suddenly offer Titan some tuna with the pill inside it, he will become suspicious and refuse ^to eat it. Try this method instead.

Make a small ball of tuna around Titan's pill. Put the tuna ball on a plate. Then find ⟨sumthing⟩ *something* you like to eat and put that on the plate, too. Take your plate and sit down at the kitchen table.

Titan will probably be watching you carefully, but you should ignore him. He's a very smart dog, and it will not be easy to fool him. your chances of success are best if you just pretend you don't see him.

Titan will soon sit beside you and start to beg. Eat your own food and continue to ignore Titan. Then, very casually, allow the ball of tuna to fall to the floor. You should make a quick grab for the tuna, but you must be sure that Titan gets to it first. Titan will eagerly gulp the tuna–and the pill.

### p. 41
1. You will need the following materials to make a Newton's cradle: a ruler marked in inches, 1 pencil or dowel rod, a pair of scissors, 5 paper clips, 5 eight-inch pieces of fishing line, and 5 wooden beads. 2. The beads must line up exactly and evenly in order to hit each other and transfer energy. 3. The fishing line holds the beads and lets them swing freely. 4. Possible response: If I could, I would build a life-sized Newton's cradle. For the frame, I would use a backyard swing set with all the swings taken off. I would use four old bowling balls as the "beads." They would all need to be the same weight, but they could be different colors. I would ask my dad to help me drill 1-inch holes through the bowling balls with his electric drill. Then, I would find a long rope 1 inch thick. I would use a yardstick to measure the rope into four 5-foot-long pieces. Then, I'd ask my dad to help me cut it. I'd use the pieces of rope to hang the bowling balls on the frame.

### p. 42
1. The writer states the purpose of the paper clearly, lists materials, and gives step-by-step instructions. 2. A Newton's cradle is used to demonstrate scientific principles. If the writer had not included the first paragraph, we might know how to make a Newton's cradle, but we wouldn't know what to do with it or

why it is interesting. 3. Listing the materials before giving the directions helps readers make sure they have everything they need before they start building the cradle. 4. The writer uses sequence words such as *first*, *next*, and *then* to help you understand the order of the steps. These words also help you find your place in the process quickly. 5. Answers may vary. Pictures should illustrate moving beads. Pictures or labels should explain the change from kinetic energy to sound and heat energy.

## Unit 3: Descriptive Writing

### p. 47
Your child underlines "Each summer Ron and Diane go to their favorite beach house– their great-aunt's beach house." Possible responses: sight: three-bedroom house, ocean in front, mountain range in back, piles of seaweed, jellyfish, blue-green water, sea lion, shadows lengthened. hearing: cuckoo clock, bark, singing. smell: dead fish. taste: none. touch: slippery, smooth shell

### p. 48
Your child underlines "The room had clearly been ransacked." 1. Possible responses: open and empty drawers, strewn clothes, empty closet, portrait of a solemn young woman–all sight. crunch of glass–hearing. fragrance of perfume, garlic–smell. broken glass underfoot–touch 2. space order; Possible answers are "next to," "trail...led," "underfoot," "on the wall."

### p. 49
Possible responses: sight: green vegetation, white sand, blue water. hearing: surf thundering, stomach growling. smell: salty smell of ocean, smoky smell of roasting pig. taste: salty water. touch: soft sands, cool water, hot sun

### p. 50
Be sure that your child includes precise words. Possible responses: 1. underline first sentence. Bob heard a loud banging at the door. 2. underline second sentence. He ran to the front door. 3. underline first sentence. A young boy was standing on the front porch. 4. underline second sentence. The girl's tears clearly showed her grief. 5. underline second sentence. "We have lost our big cat." 6. underline first sentence. "Does your cat have brown rings?" asked Bob. 7. underline second sentence. "He is curled up asleep."

### p. 51
Possible responses: 1. A small brown dog huddled in the shelter of the tunnel. 2. It shivered in the icy, penetrating wind. 3. Finally, it left the shelter of the tunnel and began to wander down the street. 4. Its dark shadow trailed behind it. 5. The dog and its shadow trotted down the street. 6. The dog broke through the thin sheet of ice on the puddle and wet its paw.

### p. 52–53
A set of smooth stone steps led up to a flat clearing in the forest⊙ Here the sun's rays filtered down through the branches of the towering pines, and the ground was covered with fragrant green pine needles. the carpet of needles felt thick and soft under Nina's feet.

a gentle breeze rustled the branches⊙ Nina inhaled the scent of the pines as it drifted on the breeze. mingled with the scent of pine was the smell of the pale green mosses growing on the north sides of the trees.

What was that in the middle of the clearing? Nina saw a large stump, just under three ⟨feat⟩ *feet* tall and a full three feet in diameter. four smaller stumps were arranged around it⊙ Paul was already seated on one of the smaller stumps, and the large stump was clearly just the right ⟨hieght⟩ *height* for a table.

On the large stump lay a basket of juicy blackberries, a canteen, and two shiny metal cups⊙ Paul looked up at Nina and asked, "Are you ready for a treat?"

### p. 61
1. The writer uses interesting words, similes, and metaphors to describe what Cole and his dad saw, heard, felt, and did. 2. Cole traced the stitching on his bag. His mom was relieved when Cole's dad telephoned. 3. The writer tells us that Cole reassures his dad that he's not upset about the late start to the weekend. Cole tells his dad that he loves the farm and the house. 4. Answers will vary. Check drawings. 5. Guide your child in summarizing the significant events of the story.

### p. 62
1. "Their red and yellow heads moved up and down like fishing bobs on a lake." "The creek babbled like a child." 2. "The highway was a gray stripe through green countryside." 3. Some interesting verbs included sliced, bowed, babbled, sparkled, swallowed, and groaned. 4. Drawings should show the interior of a farmhouse, covered with dust and spider webs. Cole should be in the room, with his dad holding his elbow. 5. Answers will vary. Look for descriptive language that expresses the five senses, comparisons, varied sentence length, and personal style, or voice.

## Unit 4: Comparative Writing

**p. 67**
1. comparison 2. contrast 3. Possible responses: intelligent, loyal, helpful, good conversationalists, excellent sense of humor 4. Possible responses: Lena complains and argues. Taylor rarely complains or argues. Lena is more honest. Taylor talks behind someone's back.

**p. 68**
1. circle: new house, old house underline: similar to, like, both, both, and so did—comparison 2. circle: new house, old house underline: different, unlike, while—contrast

**p. 69**

| Category | Rabbit A | Both rabbits | Rabbit B |
|---|---|---|---|
| 1. type of animal | | | |
| 2. shape | tall, thin | | short, plump |
| 3. clothes | | hats | |
| 4. expression | clever, shrewd | | happy |
| 5. ears | standing up | | floppy |

6. Both are rabbits; both are wearing hats.
7. Possible responses include differences in shape, expression, and ears.

**p. 70**
1. Both groups of Indians farmed and raised animals. Pueblos and Navajos also both wove cloth. 2. The Pueblos depended entirely on the crops and livestock they raised. The Navajos hunted and gathered as well as raised food and livestock. The Navajos wove wool, while the Pueblos wove cotton and feathers together.

**p. 71**
Possible responses: 1. Both water-skiing and snow skiing require skis. However, the similarity ends there. Snow skiing is a cold-weather sport. In contrast, water-skiing is a sport for warm weather. People snow ski on a mountain slope, while water-skiing is done on a large body of water. 2. I like to be moving throughout a game. Therefore, I like playing football better than playing baseball. Indeed, in football, the whole team is in motion on every play. In contrast, when a baseball team is at bat, most of the players are sitting and waiting.

**p. 72–73**
    People sometimes (asks) *ask* me who my best friend is. Truthfully, I do not know. I have two close friends, and I like them both very much.
    My friends judy and Margie (is) *are* alike in many ways. Both are intelligent, loyal, and helpful◯ Either can carry on a great conversation. Each has an excellent sense of humor, and they enjoy many of the same activities.
    However, my two friends are different in many ways. I (has) *have* more arguments with Judy. She complains if she does not like something, and she (argue) *argues* if she disagrees with me. Margie rarely complains or argues, so we almost never (fights) *fight*.
    On the other hand, Judy is a more honest friend. She always says exactly what she thinks or feels. In contrast, Margie never (say) *says* anything negative to me about things i̲ have said or done. Instead, she may say something to someone else, and her comments often (gets) *get* back to me. If Judy has a complaint, she discusses it with the person who has caused the problem.

**p. 79**
Guide your child in organizing the information in a clear manner. How In-line Skates and Ice Skates Are Alike: Both in-line skates and ice skates are built for speed.; The way skates are made today lets skaters skate well all the time.; Skates can be used in more than one sport.; The boots of both in-line and ice skates support the ankles firmly and comfortably.; Both types of skates have devices that help them move. How In-line Skates and Ice Skates Are Different: In-line skates are used on land while ice skates are made for ice.; The boots of in-line skates are made of plastic, with a liner that can be removed and washed. Ice skates, however, have boots made of leather. The lining lets air move, but it must be wiped clean each time you use the skates because it cannot be taken out.; In-line skates have wheels, usually four, which make them move. The fastest in-line skates have wheels that are bigger (about 76 mm), harder (up to 100 durometers), and have good ball bearings. Ice skates, on the other hand, use blades to move. Blades are solid metal, usually stainless steel coated with chrome, nickel, or aluminum. Each blade has a toe pick to help the skater take off and a ridge called a "hollow" that cuts the ice.; Skaters using in-line skates have brakes at the back of each boot to help them stop, but ice-skaters have to use their legs and feet to press down on the sides of their skates to stop.

**p. 80**
1. The writer introduces the topic of the paper in the first paragraph. 2. The similarities are clear and easy to explain, so the writer describes those first. 3. The first difference is how the boots of in-line skates and ice skates are made. The boots of in-line skates are usually made of firm plastic, while ice skate boots are made of leather. Another difference is that in-line skates use wheels, but ice skates use blades. The third difference is related to stopping. In-line skates have brakes, but ice skates don't. I think the writer presented the differences in this order because he or she could talk about how the boots are made, then describe how they move when you're wearing them. When you're skating, the last thing you do is stop, so it makes sense to discuss that last. 4. The first paragraph introduces the topic of the paper. The last paragraph summarizes the paper's topic.

## Unit 5: Persuasive Writing

**p. 86**
1. emotional words 2. testimonial 3. emotional words 4. faulty generalization 5. fact 6. opinion

**p. 87**
1. emotional words 2. testimonial 3. bandwagon technique 4. faulty generalization 5. emotional words 6. testimonial

**p. 88**
1. fact 2. opinion 3. opinion 4. should; opinion 5. ought; opinion 6. fact 7. fact 8. probably; opinion 9. silly; opinion 10. fact 11. fact

**p. 89**
1. How can a planet such as Theron still tolerate the disgraceful laws that permit slavery in the year 3045? 2. The Theronites should demand an end to that practice. 3. Thousand of Robots are chained to their masters by existing laws. 4. The Robots labor from dawn until midnight without pay. 5. Robot catchers are hired to track down escaping Robots. 6. To be a truly modern planet, Theron should crush out practices that deny freedom to all Theronites.

**p. 90**
Possible responses: 1. I think it is important for people to use less energy. After all, every kind of energy costs us something. Fuels made from fossils pollute the air and are in short supply. 2. Other sources of energy also have drawbacks. For example, water power requires damming rivers, sometimes destroying beautiful valleys. Even manufacturing the equipment for other sources of energy uses energy and creates pollution in the process. When we cut our use of energy, we can avoid many harmful results of our present overuse of it.

**p. 91–92**
    The people of the World are faced with alarming environmental problems. I am convinced that we must all cooperate through international (agencys) *agencies* to solve these problems. Working alone, one state or

one nation cannot protect its land and people from environmental hazards. The problems faced by people in the united states are also problems for people in canada, Japan, and russia. Only by facing these problems together and trying to work out cooperative solutions can we protect ourselves and our planet.

There are several reasons why international cooperation is needed. in the first place, some environmental dangers threaten the whole (plant) *planet* rather than local areas. Damage to the ozone layer is a good example. If someone in nebraska uses an aerosol spray, the chemicals do not stay in Nebraska. Those damaging chemicals travel to the ozone layer, where they affect the whole world. Therefore, a State or Country cannot protect itself against ozone damage simply by passing a law forbidding the local use of aerosols.

## p. 100
1. The Ogre is not your usual hero. He isn't handsome and he prefers to live alone. 2. Other important characters in the movie are Princess Stella, the moles, and Manco, the villain. 3. Bernie rescues the princess from a dragon so the moles will go back to their village and leave Bernie alone in the forest. 4. Check to see that your child identifies the purpose of the review and summarizes its significant points.

## p. 101
1. The writer outlines the elements of a fairy tale, which are familiar to everyone. Then the writer tells the reader that the characters in this fairy tale are different, making this the funniest fairy tale ever. 2. The writer doesn't want to spoil the movie for the reader, but he or she wants to share a few exciting moments to convince the reader to see the movie. 3. Most movies have people or look like cartoons. It is amazing for a computer-animated movie to look so realistic that people will want to see it. 4. In the first paragraph, the writer presents the opinion that Bernie, the Laughing Ogre is one of the funniest fairy tales ever. In the last paragraph, the writer restates the opinion and summarizes the reasons the reader should see the movie.

## Unit 6: Short Report

### p. 106
1. c 2. b 3. b 4. c 5. a

### p. 107
Possible responses; accept other supported responses:
1. body; gives a fact 2. body; gives a fact 3. introduction; gets attention 4. body; gives a fact 5. introduction; gets attention 6. body; gives a fact 7. conclusion; sums up 8. body; gives a fact 9. body; gives a fact
10. conclusion; sums up, leaves reader interested in topic

### p. 108
A. Underline 1, 2, 4, 6 B. Possible response: Young children learn through play. Wise parents and teachers provide many opportunities for a variety of play experiences.

### p. 109
Possible responses: Striking beginning: My grandfather used to threaten to make grasshopper gravy, just as other people do around the world. Concrete details: 1, 5, 6, 7, 8. Quotation: 9.

### p. 110
Possible responses: 2. During this period, the Industrial Revolution, a new society was created. 3. A spinner, James Hargreaves, invented a new spinning machine. 4. The new machine, the spinning jenny, could spin eight threads at once. 5. Edmund Cartwright invented a water-powered loom. 6. Eli Whitney invented a cotton gin in 1793.

### p. 111–112
Can you imagine an animal that seems to be part mammal, Part reptile, and part bird? If you succeed, you will probably imagine an animal very much like the duckbill, also called a platypus.

Animals that bear their young alive and nurse their young are classified As mammals. Duckbills nurse their young as mammals do, but they lay eggs as birds do. Although scientists classify the duckbill as a kind of (mammmil,) *mammal* it has characteristics of other animal groups.

In appearance, the duckbill most closely resembles a duck. like a duck, it has a large bill. it also has webbed feet, fur, and a flat tail like a beaver's.

Most mammals are warm-blooded. Their body temperature remains the same regardless of the temperature Of their surroundings. A duckbill is cold-blooded like a reptile. its body temperature changes with the temperature of its surroundings.

Duckbills die in captivity, so they must be studied in their natural homes.

### p. 119
1. Barbara was surprised because she had heard the bats make lots of sounds, including buzzes, squeals, and chirps, but she had never heard them sing like a bird before. 2. Usually, the bats liked to roost together. Sometimes they had little fights, but they always got over them quickly and made up with each other. All this made Barbara curious about why the bats were fighting more often. 3. Amanda Lollar is a licensed expert in the care of Mexican free-tailed bats like the ones Barbara kept, which means she would probably be able to answer Barbara's questions. 4. Be sure that your child identifies the report's main ideas and includes significant details. Spelling, punctuation, capitalization, and grammar should be correct.

### p. 120
1. The writer introduced the topic of the report, bats, in the first paragraph. 2. The writer lists all of the sounds that Barbara's bats usually make (chirps, buzzes, and squeals). Then the writer tells us that Barbara had never heard this song before. 3. The fifth paragraph explains how the bats usually act and tells the reader that Hank was different. In the next paragraph, the writer gives specific examples of how Hank's behavior was different from that of the other bats. 4. The first paragraph tells the reader that Barbara would make a scientific discovery. In the last paragraph, the writer explains that the behaviors Barbara observed helped scientists learn more about the bats' mating behaviors.